The Cheapskate's Guide to Weddings and Honeymoons

The Cheapskate's Guide to Weddings and Honeymoons

David W. Shaw

A Citadel Press Book
Published by Carol Publishing Group

Carol Publishing Group Edition, 1997

A Citadel Press Book
Published by Carol Publishing Group
Citadel Press is a registered trademark of Carol Communications, Inc.

Editorial, sales and distribution, rights and permissions inquiries
should be addressed to Carol Publishing Group, 120 Enterprise Avenue,
Secaucus, N.J. 07094

In Canada: Canadian Manda Group, One Atlantic Avenue, Suite 105,
Toronto, Ontario M6K 3E7

Carol Publishing Group books may be purchased in bulk at special
discounts for sales promotions, fund-raising, or educational purposes.
Special editions can be created to specifications. For details, contact
Special Sales Department, Carol Publishing Group, 120 Enterprise Avenue,
Secaucus, N.J. 07094

Manufactured in the United States of America
10 9 8 7 6 5 4 3 2

The advice contained in this book is meant to serve as a guide, but ultimately
the decisions you make about your wedding and honeymoon are your own.
Neither the author or publisher can be held responsible for any difficulties,
financial or otherwise, which may arise.

Library of Congress Cataloging-in-Publication Data

Shaw, David, 1943–
    The cheapskate's guide to weddings and honeymoons / David Shaw.
        p.   cm.
    "A Citadel Press book."
    ISBN 0-8065-1838-3 (pbk.)
    1. Weddings—United States—Planning. 2. Honeymoon—United
    States—Planning. 3. Consumer education—United States. I. Title.
HQ745.S45   1996
395'.22—dc20   96-34150
                                                                    CIP

For my wife and best friend, Elizabeth,
with all my love for a marriage
made in heaven.

Contents

**CHAPTER 14   Flowers: Finding Your Way
                       Through the Financial Weeds   76**

*The flowers you'll need • Average costs • The much
cheaper nursery • When and how to get started •
Cost-saving tips*

CHAPTER 15   The Music   83

*Setting the mood • Music for the ceremony • Choosing
music for the reception • Bands and DJs • Prices and
ways to save • About booking agencies*

CHAPTER 16   Photographs for Posterity   91

*Average costs • Cost-saving tips • How to find and choose
a photographer • On film formats • The photojournalist
approach*

CHAPTER 17   Video and Your Wedding   97

*Video, the latest trend • Video prices and packages •
Tips from a video expert*

CHAPTER 18   Cheapskate Weddings   103

*Chapel weddings • Weddings at home • Small
weddings*

CHAPTER 19   All About Wedding Consultants 108

*What the consultant does • Tips from the
Association of Bridal Consultants*

Part II: Saving Money on Your Honeymoon

CHAPTER 20   The Sweetest Time   117

*Honeymoons today...the super vacation Honeymoon
traditions • Average price of a honeymoon •
Importance of staying on budget*

Acknowledgments

I want to thank everyone who gave so freely of their time to share information and insights for this book. To list every name isn't possible, but here are a few individuals I would greatly like to thank.

Foremost are Steven Schragis, Gary Fitzgerald, and Kevin McDonough for their involvement behind the scenes at Carol Publishing. I also want to thank Patricia Kaneb, Priscilla of Boston; Eileen Monaghan, Association of Bridal Consultants; Bob and Jo Ann Mehaffey, Mehaffey Multimedia Productions; Janine Sylvestro, PJ's Towne Florist; Wayne Smith, National Limousine Association; and Admiral Pat Theberge, Cruise Vacations.

Author's Note

I'm not ashamed to admit I'm the ultimate cheapskate. People have teased me about my Scottish thrift for years, and I don't mind. It's just my philosophy not to pay more than necessary—ever! And to not spend money I don't have.

Take my wedding for instance. When my wife and I got married in 1987, we couldn't afford a formal wedding with all the frills. So, instead of going into debt for it, we asked a friend who was mayor of a small town to marry us, and he did on Halloween. For free, too. Only our best man and matron-of-honor, and my bride's son from a previous marriage attended.

After the ceremony, my wife and I drove to a fancy restaurant on the Jersey shore, which also had a handful of small but nice rooms overlooking the sea, where we dined with my mother and a friend of hers. They bought dinner and paid for our modest bridal suite. The next day, we went back to work. The following summer, we went camping for our honeymoon.

Now I know most of you don't want a wedding or honeymoon like that, even if you are as broke as I was when I got married. I know you're not too keen on going into debt, either. So what do you do?

After witnessing the mental and emotional mayhem friends have gone through trying to have a wedding and honeymoon without going broke, and after writing about weddings and travel for years, I felt it was high time to write a book to help brides and grooms through the financial mine field.

Presto! Here we are with *The Cheapskate's Guide to Weddings and Honeymoons*.

In a nutshell, this book was written to show you how to have a great traditional wedding and honeymoon without going to the poor house. It'll help you make decisions along the way that can save thousands of dollars, and you won't come off like the ultimate cheapskate or sacrifice quality for low prices on inferior goods and services.

Along with information on trends, prices for products and services, wedding etiquette and planning, and names and numbers of providers to take some of the work out of the process, the book will take you into a philosophy which enables you to turn basic business principles in your favor. Weddings and honeymoons are big business, and a businesslike approach makes sense when deciding how to spend thousands of hard-earned dollars.

Good luck in planning a special wedding and honeymoon, and enjoy the celebration and the memories!

PART I

Saving Money on Your Wedding

CHAPTER

1

The Leap of Faith

Weddings have long been social events. Whole communities used to gather together and join in the celebration befitting a couple throwing their lots together to live as one for the rest of their lives. Apart from the celebratory aspect, a wedding is a public affirmation of love between two people.

The roots of the word "wedding" stem from Anglo-Saxon usage meaning pledge. The pledge of marriage has always been taken seriously, representing the core of family and community. It's a big step, one which causes excitement and anxiety, and tugs at the strings of tradition dating back to the dawn of time.

More than 2.3 million people get married every year in the United States, roughly one percent of the population. Every year, all those folks getting married spend $11 billion dollars just for wedding day celebrations. This figure takes in such things as receptions, music, flowers, gowns, transportation, photography, and many other categories.

Pre- and postwedding day expenditures for showers, parties, invitations, rehearsal dinners, furnishings, new homes or apartment rentals, honeymoons, and other items add an additional $21 billion to the revenue spent for weddings during a one-year period in the United States. That's a grand annual total of $32 billion.

As you can see, weddings are big business. You're about to sweeten the pot with some of your hard-earned cash, so going into the planning process with as much information as you can gather makes good sense. Your wedding isn't like buying stocks or a home, but it still must be considered as a significant investment. It will pay dividends and build equity in an intangible sense, yet one which is of equal or more value than mere dollars and cents.

All too often, however, the groom will pop the question, the bride will say yes, and together the couple will set a date without much knowledge about all that goes into a wedding. Caught up in the moment, they pick a date which appeals to them—usually it's a spring or early fall date regardless of where they live.

Only after the job of planning the wedding begins do they realize how important the date really is from a financial stand-point, and how it can make or break limited budgets. Very few young couples select dates with any consideration of finances; it's an emotional decision, and that can cost a lot of money.

The reception accounts for the largest share of the overall budget for a wedding. Selecting a date in the peak wedding season will mean higher costs for the reception in most cases. Popular ceremony and reception sites are booked up for at least a year in advance. The couple often must scramble to find a good one on the special date they chose without thinking ahead.

Thus, without knowing it, the couple who select a date without considering the financial implications has placed themselves at the mercy of the wedding industry, which, like every other business, works on the basic principle of supply and demand. When demand is high, so are prices for just about everything associated with the day. Instead of having the advantage of a buyer's market, the couple is faced with beating the odds of a seller's market.

For someone concerned about budget, this is a very real

problem. Tips on the least expensive dates, times of the week, and times of day for weddings will follow in the next chapters. But first let's look at timing, budget, current trends, and other options key to getting the show on the road.

Timing

Ideally, you'll have a year in which to plan the ceremony and reception as well as the honeymoon. Time is your best friend. As a rule, the less time you have the more money you'll spend. When you're in a hurry, you won't take the time to shop around, to play the discount game, to go into each phase with enough information and a clear idea of what you want and are willing to pay. You also won't have time to do the extra work necessary to save money by reducing labor costs, which comprise a hefty share of the overall expenses.

If you don't have a year to plan the wedding, that's okay, though considering a later date would be to your advantage. Yet, nothing in life is ever ideal, even marriage. If you have limited time, go into the process knowing that less time reduces your ability to get the best wedding and honeymoon at the lowest possible price without compromising too much on quality services and products. This book will help you even the odds, just the same.

An average couple planning a traditional wedding and reception for 100 guests or more spends a minimum of 100 hours on the process according to estimates from the Association of Bridal Consultants. The total number of hours required often exceeds the minimum figure when travel times to the various service and product providers, telephone calls, addressing invitations, and other tasks involved are figured into the equation. The saving grace: if you can spread out the time in little pieces versus in giant blocks, the hours you spend will be less demanding and less stressful.

Budget

The typical formal wedding, if there is such a thing, will have a budget for services and products broken down into the following broad categories. The range of the percentages within the total budget for each should provide a useful guide. The budget doesn't include items such as engagement rings, attire for parents of the bride and groom, rehearsal site and dinner, bridal luncheons, and other costs before the wedding.

Hypothetical total budget: $10,000   Don't worry if you don't have the $10,000. I have chosen this figure because it represents a national average spent for a semiformal or formal wedding with a sit-down dinner reception for one hundred guests. Bridal magazines put the figure at closer to $16,000 for a wedding involving slightly more guests.

At $10,000, the math for each budget category will be easy to calculate at a glance. The breakdown will provide you with a basic idea of prices for each category, though they vary from region to region.

Wedding rings	2 to 5 percent
Wedding stationery: Invitations, announcements, thank-you notes, programs	3 percent
Ceremony: Officiant fee, site fee, musicians	3 to 6 percent
Transportation	5 percent
Reception: Site, food, liqour	30 to 40 percent
Music	5 to 20 percent
Photographer	10 to 15 percent
Flowers	7 to 10 percent
Bridal gown and accessories	8 to 10 percent
Groom's attire	1 to 3 percent

Miscellaneous: 26 percent
    Can include aisle runner, favors,
    souvenirs, guest book, jewelry,
    trousseau, gifts for attendants,
    videos, wedding consultants, and
    other categories

Assuming you have $10,000 to spend on the wedding and reception, not an usual sum these days, you'll have that $2,600 left under miscellaneous to channel into other categories if you calculated the minimum percentages for the rest. In addition, some of the categories have a great deal of leeway for adjustments, which will be covered in subsequent chapters.

Although prices vary widely from site to site and state to state, $30 per plate setting for a catered dinner isn't uncommon. If you have one hundred guests, you'll likely spend at least $3,000 for the meal, not including service charges, gratuities, and liqour. In the Northeastern states, California, and other more populated locations in the country, catered reception dinners at fancy places can start at $60.00 per place setting even in the off-season.

For our hypothetical wedding budget, spending $6,000 on the meal amounts to 60 percent of the total expenses! That's way too much. You still might swing it if all the other categories fall in line with minimum percentages, but they won't and you'll have to cut corners elsewhere. Cutting them won't make sense if one portion of the budget is out of whack.

Would it make sense to spend 60 percent of the total budget on the reception at the cost of hiring limousines for you and the wedding party? Arriving at a fancy dinner in a VW microbus or a rusty pickup embodies a touch of the absurd. Likewise, would you eliminate a professional photographer at such a reception in favor of Aunt Jane with a trusty Polaroid camera?

If you have to have that $60 per plate setting, you'd do better to cut the guest list in half to fall back into a reasonable percentage. Or find a less expensive reception site and menu to keep the balance in the budget. As you can see from these hypothetical examples, the type of reception and the total number of guests comprise two of the most important considerations. You'll find you're looking for balance throughout the planning process, and finding it will require flexibility and a willingness to compromise.

What if you don't have ten grand to plunk down? That's where time, creativity, flexibility, and just plain good horse sense really come in. The tighter the budget, the more you'll have to make difficult choices. But there is always a way to come out ahead and still have a great wedding day. As the expression goes, there is more than one way to skin a cat.

The above figures are meant to give you a broad idea of where whatever cash you've got is going to go. All wedding professionals agree the reception eats up the most cash, but there are many different kinds of receptions and ways of handling them. These will be discussed in the chapter under that heading.

The important point to keep in mind is that the budget will cover a large number of categories. Familiarize yourself with them, then decide what's important to you and your families. After that, it's time to start getting estimates for all categories, plus subcategories. Add them up and compare the total cost against what you have to spend. Once you've started that you're really on your way.

Planning a wedding has been compared to running a corporation, directing a movie, or commanding a military operation. All these comparisons share one premise in common: Sound management and deployment of resources spell success.

CHAPTER
2

Trends in the 1990s

In the 1980s, weddings in general were more garish and loaded with all the trappings of pomp and wealth, partly because many young couples and their families had more disposable income. The yuppie was in full glory and would settle on nothing but the best and most expensive type of formal wedding.

At the time, six-piece bands were common. DJs were considered cheap blue-collar forms of entertainment for weddings. Gowns were more decked out with beads, exhorbitantly priced imported lace, and other complicated design features which cost a fortune. Synthetic fabrics were considered cheap and no self-respecting yuppie would even think of buying a gown with an inch of that fake stuff.

The ostentatious tendencies of the 1980s reflected the mood of the nation as it rode the wave of hyper-economic activity which cut across virtually all industries from stocks to real estate. The reasons why aren't important for this book, but suffice it to say popular trends in weddings often are reflective of the overall feelings people have about their country's health and of their own futures.

Today, with fears of job security, shrinking incomes, stagnating wages, and uncertainty about the future both for individuals and for the nation, some of the flashy touches so popular in the last decade have been abandoned in favor of a more laid-back, though still elegant approach to weddings. DJs are now common even at upscale weddings. Gowns are still elegant, but in simpler ways. Invitations have gotten less gaudy. The times indeed have been a-changin'.

The simple wedding at home with a justice of the peace also has been gaining in popularity, as have destination weddings where the couple travels with a small wedding party to some exotic spot, gets married, and starts the honeymoon right away.

Apart from the economic issues, many weddings of the 1990s are being driven by the disconnectedness of contemporary American life. Fewer and fewer couples have firm roots in one place for long periods, nor do they have long-term attachments to churches or other religious organizations, partly because of the highly mobile nature of society. This helps account for the rise of simpler weddings and the increased popularity of the justice of the peace approach. It's easy and there are no hassles with interfaith, interracial, and intercultural marriages.

However, some things change more slowly than others. There are a lot of Victorian trappings in today's weddings such as the dedication to white, virginal gowns. (White didn't begin to gain popularity as a color for gowns until the late 1700s, and bloomed in the twentieth century.)

The traditions for weddings which have evolved over the ages, particularly in the last several centuries, tend to place most of the financial and planning responsibilities on the bride and her family. This no doubt arose from the notion that marrying off the daughter was in the interest of the bride's family, since spinsters placed a permanent financial burden on their families.

In fact, the word bridal stems from the practice of the bride's family selling bride's-ale on the wedding day to help cover costs. Hence, bride's-ale became the bridal of today.

Traditionally, the bride's father was and still is supposed to pay most of the expenses for the wedding. The bride, her mother, and her friends get the pleasure of seeing to most every detail to make the wedding and reception go smoothly. The groom pays for a small part of the wedding such as gifts for attendants, some of the flowers, the officiant's fee and all of the honeymoon. The groom's parents also kick in cash for the rehearsal dinner and other minor things.

However, traditions haven't kept pace with reality in the mid-1990s. Brides today often have full-time jobs and work as hard as the grooms. Her friends who will be in the bridal party also work, and her mother probably does, too. Many couples just don't have the time to plan their weddings, so they hire wedding consultants.

For the couple going it alone, the lack of time available means that whatever moments can be carved out of busy schedules to plan a successful wedding will be at a premium. The groom can't sit idle as he once could, leaving it all up to the women. Today's grooms are more in touch with the process. They know enough to get involved and stay involved, offering a helping hand to their brides-to-be. A partnership, after all, is what makes a good marriage. Planning the wedding should be a good practice run at the real thing.

Together, the bride and groom in the mid-1990s face the reality that the old ways of sharing the work involved in a wedding are changing. Duties have to be spread out and better coordinated. For example, the groom's friends should help with getting price estimates and other tasks like addressing or stuffing invitations. It's not "women's work" anymore. It may not be easy to get the groom's friends involved, but today every hand is needed and the groom needs to realize that and do something about it.

And then there's the big question of money…who's going to pay for all this?

Today an increasing number of couples are sharing costs with parents and relatives or paying for the whole affair themselves. The trend stems from simple economics and other factors.

Weddings of the past were more affordable partly because dollars went farther. Today, a formal wedding and a sit-down dinner reception for 150 guests costs a small fortune. Even a modest formal wedding and reception can easily cost in excess of $10,000.

Added to the economic changes, an increasing number of couples are putting marriage off till their mid to late twenties, and early thirties. They are strong wage earners by then and parents feel less responsible for paying the entire bill when the bride and groom together are doing well financially.

Also, parents are farther along in their work lives when the big day comes, which means paying for a wedding might well be at the cost of hard-earned retirement dollars. They may have already laid out tens of thousands for college tuitions for you and your siblings. In short, it may not be realistic, or fair, to expect parents to pay for the entire wedding.

All this boils down to some tough choices for the bride and groom. Wedding planning will require walking a tightrope to keep costs down without sacrificing too much on quality.

Sometimes, you'll do better to throw tradition out the window rather than make yourself crazy trying to stick to rigid rules of etiquette, all of which cost money. More and more couples are finding this out and are doing their own thing, from writing their own ceremonies to sending invitations as prizes in empty Cracker Jack boxes instead of spending $300 or $400 on fancy stationery.

The Guest List

No matter what kind of ceremony you decide on, the more guests invited, the more costly the reception.

The guest list is the stickiest part of planning a wedding because emotions tend to get in the way. No one wants to hurt a family member or close friend's feelings by excluding them from the event. Yet, in most cases, when the couple plans a wedding, someone inevitably must get left out to keep costs within reason.

Determining the total number of guests should be one of the very first steps in the planning process. Once you've figured out the size of the guest list, you can move on to consider the various styles of ceremonies and, most importantly, receptions. To a large extent, the size of the guest list will dictate the style of the reception a couple can afford and whether the wedding will be formal, semiformal, or informal.

In most cases, you don't have an informal wedding with two hundred guests. This is somewhat silly, since a wedding is a very personal thing. No one says a big informal ceremony with a pig roast reception can't be done; it is, in fact, quite a popular type of wedding in certain parts of the country.

But usually the desire to stick with traditions exerts a strong pull and most guests who attend a big wedding don't expect to come in blue jeans and eat a pig on a spit. Part of what makes a wedding special for many couples is the following of traditions which cover virtually every facet of the day from garters to cake.

The first step in planning the wedding must by necessity start with finances. At least that's often said. However, knowing you have X dollars to spend on the wedding and reception won't help much if you don't first decide what kind of wedding and reception you both want and how many guests you want to invite to both.

Some Wedding and Reception Options

The following options will be discussed in subsequent chapters. They are listed here to start you thinking about them as you learn more about how to shave dollars off the entire wedding process.

- Justice of the peace (no reception)
- Justice of the peace (restaurant or at-home reception)
- Home wedding and reception (can be very nice, semiformal with no reception site rental costs)

- The early-bird ceremony, breakfast or brunch reception (can be very nice, semiformal, inexpensive meal with no bills for hard liquor, bartenders, security, etc.)
- The mid-afternoon ceremony and reception (can be very nice, semiformal with no full-course meal expenses, and hard liquor need not be served)
- The late afternoon ceremony and cocktail reception (can be very nice, formal or semiformal with no full-course meal expenses)
- The late afternoon or early evening ceremony with reception (can be very nice, formal or semiformal with buffet meal)
- The late afternoon or early evening ceremony with reception (can be very nice, formal or semiformal with sit-down meal)
- Ceremonies and weddings can also be held outdoors at state or national parks, mansions, wineries, restaurants, farms, zoos—virtually anywhere. However, keep in mind that they aren't necessarily cheaper than indoor weddings.

By far the most expensive ceremony and reception is the formal style with a full sit-down dinner. While this type of wedding used to be the dream of many, today's couples are reflecting the national trend for a simpler way to approach their special day.

For example, the formal ceremony complete with van-loads of flowers, the elegant bridal gown, limousines, photography and video with a cocktail reception and no dinner, and a DJ instead of a five-piece band is becoming more accepted. Instead of a minimum of $3,000 for food for one hundred guests and $1,500 to $3,500 for a live band, an open bar and a $500 DJ (the national average for DJ service) allows the couple to channel limited cash into the other budget categories which combine to make the day special for everyone.

The style of wedding you choose is personal and related to your tastes, dreams, and the size of your budget. Just bear in mind that the social forces which once pushed Dad into spending a small fortune are now directed more at couples footing the bill, and couples in this day and age are coming up with all sorts of twists on the old traditions.

CHAPTER
3

Cost-Saving Seasons

She's as pretty as a June bride. How many times have you heard that? It's become ingrained in the American lexicon to denote beauty and the wholesome innocence of youthful love. The June bride got her fame as far back as Roman times when the goddess, Juno, wife of Jupiter, was honored during the month of June. Romans figured getting married when Juno was happy meant the bride and groom would prosper.

But for the hardy New Englanders who first settled the Northeast, and for those who traveled westward across the Appalachians to the wide plains of the Heartland, Roman gods and goddesses were as far from their minds as space travel. Yet the June bride still took her place in the collective fabric of national consciousness.

For these folks, the winter season meant hunger and death at worst and the occasional bout of cabin fever at best. Cooped up on farms or in small towns, the pace of life slowed to a crawl until the spring thaw came and the work in the fields drew the men and women back outdoors to continue the cycle of survival. Busting sod, planting and harvesting, the laying up of foods—dried, canned, pickled or otherwise preserved— for those long cold days just over the horizon as another winter approached, filled life from sunup to sundown.

The month of June came to symbolize good times when the living was easier. Although weddings occurred during most every month, the time just after spring climaxed in a blaze of blooms and before the summer solstice on June 21 held, and still holds, a very special appeal to couples planning a marriage. In the Northeast it still ranks as one of the most popular wedding months. The longer days and relatively nice weather account for this, now and in the past.

Our June bride also made it to the south and to the Pacific coast, despite the fact that winter snows posed no major bother except in the northwestern reaches of the nation and in the mountains. In some parts of the country every month is nice for a wedding from a weather standpoint. In others, June in the warmer climes isn't as popular a wedding month as it is where winter makes an obvious appearance every year.

There is another old saying worth noting: Marry in the month of June, life will be one long honeymoon.

The popularity of a given month or day for weddings has a direct impact on costs. If you want to be a June bride in regions where many other brides want the same, get ready to pay big bucks for the privilege. Also, you'd better book your ceremony and reception site at least a year in advance. The most popular locations are sometimes booked even farther in advance than that.

It's odd, but true. People go crazy about certain months and certain days of the week, and they cough up exhorbitant fees to get what they want. Of course, paying more isn't strange to them. They probably didn't even think about it. But for a couple interested in the cheapskate approach, this is exactly the kind of herdlike mentality you want to avoid.

Throughout the wedding process, be aware of the impact supply and demand will have on prices. Gowns, flowers, bands and DJs, caterers, reception halls, limousine services, bartenders and waitresses, security personnel, all are subject to the influence of supply and demand. If the service providers can charge more when demand is high, they do. If they can charge the same price when demand is low, they will, if they can get away with it. Altruism isn't a big part of making money; it never has been and it's never likely to be.

In fact, you may have to pin the providers down. Ask if they lower prices in off-peak times. If so, how much? What are you really saving? You might be surprised at how much or how little, and the answer will either tell you to keep shopping around or that your wedding won't cost all that much more in-season. To a large extent, it depends on where you live. In California, for example, wedding prices remain pretty stable year-round. In the New York metropolitan area, in Chicago, and in Nashville, demand goes up and down.

The rule of thumb is that supply and demand does play a big role in determining prices for most couples planning a wedding. It's the love that counts, not when it's made official and celebrated. Why pay more for a June wedding when one in November may cost as much as forty to fifty percent less for some of the major budget categories?

In the Northeast, upper Midwest, and the Northwest, April, May, June, September and October are the most popular wedding months. Spring and early fall weather make nice weddings. Summer weddings are also popular, though many couples prefer other times due to heat, humidity, and the fact that many guests may have vacations planned.

Of course, a January wedding in Chicago, while it can be cheaper than a June wedding because of lower reception costs, may coincide with a blizzard. That wouldn't be nice at all, though in the olden days people believed the couple would receive a dollar for every flake of snow which fell on the bride and that snow on the wedding day foretold of a happy marriage.

What's life without a little risk? Life, like marriage, is a gamble. The true cheapskate will weigh the odds carefully and always err on the side of practicality when choosing a wedding month and date. It's not easy to be practical at such an emotional time, but that's where the savings lie. A clear head and a willingness to be flexible can save thousands of dollars.

In the South, the opposite is true in terms of popular wedding months. January weddings are quite popular. From January through May, the wedding business hums along. It drops off during the summer heat, as do prices, and picks up again in September and October.

4

Cost-Saving Days

Because most people must work, couples plan weekend weddings so as many guests as possible can attend. Saturday is the most popular day no matter where you live and no matter what month you choose for the wedding. This leaves Sunday for recuperation if guests overcelebrate, as they so often do.

As explained, when demand is high, prices will be steeper. A wedding held during the week can save you as much as 40 to 50 percent on your reception hall and catering. You'll also have your pick of dates and times for both the ceremony and reception site. In fact, a weekday affair might make it possible to schedule the event in the more popular months, such as June, and to go with more formal frills.

One other factor to consider with the weekday or weeknight wedding: it may reduce the number of guests who can attend, saving costs that way, too.

A wedding held on a Friday is a good alternative to consider. Rates are lower on Fridays than on Saturdays. With a Friday celebration, you won't be competing as much for dates and times at ceremony site locations, and the same goes for the reception hall and catering. Sundays are slightly less expensive than Saturdays.

Here's one example of how you can win playing the supply

and demand game: At a posh hotel, in the affluent town of Morristown, New Jersey, the price for a sit-down dinner per person at peak (in-season on weekends) costs between $80 and $100. On a Friday, however, the price per plate setting for the same meal drops by $30 per person! If you're having one hundred guests that's a savings of $3000 right there!

Of course, if you're able to spend around $100 per plate setting at the reception, you're probably not at all concerned about a paltry $3,000. The point is that the same price breaks exist in less expensive places because of lower demand on a Friday evening for service compared to a Saturday evening. When you think about it, this is logical and sound from a business perspective since the providers like to be busy as much of the time as possible.

In the rush and excitement of planning a wedding, it's easy for couples to overlook basic business principles. Your family may press you for a more expensive time, too. Everyone offers advice, and it's easy to just throw up your hands and give in. Watch for this "pressure syndrome" and work to extricate yourself from it as diplomatically as possible. This applies to virtually every phase of wedding preparations.

Shop around and know enough to explore how to make basic economics work for you instead of against you. When you start to investigate pricing for your reception, ask places that require you to use their catering services if you get a break on Fridays. If hiring a private catering service, it won't hurt to ask when the provider's rates are at rock bottom. Some won't admit there is any fluctuation, but others will.

CHAPTER
5

Cost-Saving Times

Whether you get married in a church, synagogue, or any other location, the time of day you choose will have a direct impact on the cost of the reception to follow. Church or temple ceremonies must be held at times which don't interfere with regular services. For example, a mid-morning Sunday ceremony and a brunch reception might not be an option for some couples because their church will be occupied mid-morning on Sunday.

The brunch reception is very economical, however, compared to an evening one. See if a Saturday morning ceremony and brunch will work.

Balance and compromise are key. How much are you willing to pay for a church wedding? The desire for a church or synagogue wedding adds to the cost of the reception because there is high demand for ceremony dates and times at houses of worship during popular periods. This in turn translates to high demand for reception sites during the same periods.

Avoiding the church or synagogue ceremony makes sense from a practical standpoint if having one means getting channeled into a high demand time for reception locations. But for many, a church or synagogue wedding is a must, and that's fine. Just think about choosing a time which isn't as sought after, say during the work week, a Friday evening, a Saturday morning or an early afternoon.

The morning, midday, or afternoon ceremony gives you flexibility on what type of reception you have. You're less boxed into having to pay for meals. If you time it right, you won't have to pay for a full meal, just for things like hors d'oeuvres or finger sandwiches.

Another consideration is to have an afternoon ceremony and a cocktail-only reception that ends before the dinner hour. An evening ceremony, say at seven o'clock, and a cocktail reception with light fare is another option. Guests will know they have to eat before coming to the ceremony and reception, provided you indicate in your reception invitations that dinner won't be served, just light snacks.

Your wedding will be expensive enough as it is. If you can avoid paying for a full meal, you'll have more money to spend on other things to make your day special. It's worth some thought to consider times of day which will give you a way out, don't you think?

6

Winning the Discount Game

Retail Sales, Catalogs

Smart shoppers routinely restrict their purchases to store sales, store sale catalogs, or mail-order companies with good rates. Bridal shops often have sales in the off-season on their product lines. Buying a gown off the rack at an added discount in a store sale will save hundreds of dollars.

Buying a pair of white or off-white pumps, flats, or dyeable footwear on sale at factory outlets or retail stores is another way to save. (You can wear the pumps or flats in the summer, too, so you're not hit with buying shoes you'll wear only once.)

You can watch for sales of liquor and foods such as bulk frozen shrimp and other items for weddings at home or partially catered receptions where you supply some of the menu. You can buy potted plants which can be used for reception decorations, gifts for attendants and the bride's trousseau (special clothes and lingerie). The sky is the limit.

The store sale and catalogs will win just a tiny part of the discount game, but every penny counts. The real savings come from individual deals with service and product providers with whom you will establish a business relationship.

Wheeling and Dealing for Special Discounts

Everyone likes a bargain. Couples planning a wedding are no exception. However, in many cases the multitude of details and inexperience lead couples to settle on the first or second thing that comes down the pike. They'll go to the phone book and make some calls to get prices, and that's that. They'll also talk to friends for referrals of service and product providers.

The phone book and referrals are good ways to go about getting the estimates needed to fill out the budget categories with real numbers. But taking that route won't guarantee that you get the lowest price. In fact, the service providers will all have similar rates for similar services. The market during peak or off-season times will determine average rates.

Some providers are bound to undercut their competitors, but it won't be by much or you should be suspicious. Shopping around for the best price must be balanced against quality and professionalism. The old saying, "You get what you pay for," holds true. It's best to go with providers with rates fairly close to the average you find in your particular market rather than to go with a provider who's obviously offering a deal which sounds too good to be true.

The cheapskate approach doesn't mean you'll accept the risk of using a sloppy, unreliable, and unprofessional provider or of buying inferior products. It's more a philosophy of wedding planning based on a good grasp of business and turning the basic principles to your advantage.

With that in mind, when you start making all those telephone calls from the phone book and from referrals, ask the providers about any discounts or special deals which might be worked out between both parties. When you walk into a retail store, you're not likely to ask the clerk to knock 10 percent off the price. But when you're dealing with a service provider such as a florist, photographer, or caterer, you can ask if they'll be willing to work out a deal.

All businesses work on a profit margin. In the service trade, providers have a certain degree of flexibility in determining what margin of profits hits their "comfort zone." Realizing that, the business with a high margin may be willing to reduce it somewhat to ensure a steady cash flow. That's where you can win the game; don't blindly accept the price you're given because it may not necessarily be carved in granite.

You'd be surprised at how most people hate to ask for a discount or a special deal which might entail added services or products for the same price, extras that count as much as cash if you can get the provider to furnish them for free when they would ordinarily charge a fee. It's a little like buying a car, especially a used one. Most people hate to haggle because it makes them uncomfortable.

Due to inexperience and the discomfort which comes from haggling, most young couples simply don't approach the acquisition of services and products from a business perspective, like a purchasing agent in a big company. They're used to being passive consumers instead of realizing the power of their money can work for them.

Be honest and savvy enough to say "Hey, if I sign on for this, can you cut me a break of, say, ten percent?"

The provider might answer "No, I'm sorry. My rates are firm."

Then you counter with "What if I pay you more of a deposit up front? Or for the whole deal in advance? You'll have use of more money for a longer time. Can we work out a lower overall rate or can you add some extras to the package?

"How about waiving interest? If that's not possible, can we delay interest payments?"

Some bridal shops will take an order and start charging interest on the unpaid balance right away; others will defer it. Interest of 20 percent on a $1,000 gown, not to mention additional accessories, amounts to $200 if it takes a year to pay it off. Quibbling over interest may at first seem to be too much of a cheapskate approach, but remember, it's the little things that add up. One of the keys to having a great wedding and honeymoon at the lowest possible cost is to take advantage of the cumulative effect of saving small amounts here and there any way you can.

The providers will consider your questions about discounts, special deals, and waived or deferred interest, particularly if there is a lot of money being spent with them. If he or she is an entrepreneur, the answer is likely to be yes. Your best bet is to deal with the owners of small local companies in your area; the bigger the operation, the more red tape and the less likely you'll be able to negotiate with a decision maker.

A caveat: offering advance payment should be done only when you've got the cash to front, when sure about the provider, when the discount or added services are truly worth it, and only with a solid contract to back up the verbal agreement. The example of this kind of back and forth is meant to illustrate the point that business is fluid, and often there is room to work out a better deal. Most couples just accept what they're told and never think to negotiate.

The worst that can happen is that the provider says no. Then you've got a choice to accept their rates or to keep shopping around to find a better deal or confirm that the price you were offered really was pretty good for what you're receiving. If you don't ask, the provider's not going to offer any special discount.

If you don't feel able to wheel and deal, get the price estimates and qualify the providers as hot prospects. When you're ready to close a deal, get a family member who's been around a spell and knows how to negotiate to close it for you. Some parents, grandparents, uncles, aunts, or other family members may be just what the doctor ordered.

The Nonhaggling Way to Receive Special Discounts

Perhaps you just can't find it in your heart to ask for discounts and negotiate for them with reluctant providers. One great way to get discounts without haggling is through ads in a newspaper's wedding section. Most major papers have them, and they feature ads from local providers eager for business. They wouldn't advertise if they didn't want new business for the future.

Many of the ads will offer a coupon or a discount. The discount will usually be a percentage off the providers' rates for services, or off their products. Other ads will say the provider offers discount packages. Take advantage of these offers. The savings can add up to a handsome sum when you spread them across all the budget categories.

To find out if major papers in your area have wedding ad sections, give their classified or advertising department a call to inquire. If they do, order a back issue. When you call the providers tell them you have a coupon or an ad offering a discount. Many will honor the discount even if it has expired. Those that won't don't want your business badly enough. Find someone who does.

Some more populated states, where there is enough economic activity to support them, have regional bridal guides. These are advertiser-driven, meaning a small amount of editorial content nests with a multitude of ads from wedding service and product providers.

Many of the ads will feature prices for various packages. This will help define early on the market rates in your area without making lots of phone calls to start with. The ads also will occasionally offer price or percentage discounts. Usually, you have to mention the ad to receive them. This makes sense from the provider's view; he or she wants to know if the money spent on the ad is paying off in good response totals.

To find out if these guides exist in your area, contact a wedding consultant, local bridal shops, reception sites, and other wedding industry professionals listed in the phone book. Travel agencies with experience in honeymoons are also a good bet.

Ads in national bridal magazines are great from an informational standpoint. They can tell you much about the different brands of products and types of services available. *Modern Bride* magazine and *Bride's* magazine, the two major bridal publications on the market, have regional issues with regional ad sections. *Modern Bride*, for instance, has *ten* regional breakout for *each* issue! These carry ads from reception sites, caterers, bridal salons and formal wear stores, limousine services, DJ services, and many others.

7

Dealing With Salespeople

Some salespeople are very nice, others are pushy. Some are honest and others aren't. You'll run across all kinds before you're off enjoying your honeymoon. The wedding planning process is a lot of hard work, and it's time-consuming. It will be tempting to cave into salespeople who are slick about upselling couples undecided on what they really want or anxious to just get on with their plans. After all, most of these salespeople have had lots of experience in the wedding biz. It's their bread and butter, their job. You're new at the game and are an easy mark. Remember that.

Go into any sales situation as well-armed as possible with information about the service or product beforehand. Know what you want. That's different from calling to see what providers can offer, hoping they'll tell you what you want.

Read bridal magazines to learn about the different types of gowns, headpieces, and other accessories. Once you've got a good idea of what you want, you can focus on how to get it at the lowest possible price. You'll be less likely to find yourself steered into more expensive options.

For example, if you're having a buffet reception you know chicken is one of the least expensive meats. When you call local catering services or reception sites which offer catering as a package, ask right away what kinds of chicken dishes are available. Cut to the chase, as they say. That kind of focus saves time and money.

It's okay to ask questions of salespeople. That's what they're paid for. But be up front with them and outline your budget and expectations right away. Don't let them swing you up to more expensive services or products. They'll try. And the best ones will do it so you hardly even notice.

The way you handle sales situations is an indirect method of saving money on your wedding, but it's one of the most important. The wedding industry is big business. The players know their profession and are willing to help, but they can only do that if you know what you want. Always remember, the more money you spend with them, the happier they will be. Only you have your best interests at heart.

CHAPTER
8

The Importance Of Contracts

It's a shame the days are over when a handshake and a promise could be relied on. That sort of trust, however, no longer lives in today's business world. When you decide to use a provider of a service or product, get all the details required of them, and you, in writing.

Contracts are pretty routine in the wedding industry. Caterers, reception halls, bridal shops, makeup salons, florists, DJs and bands, photographers, limousine services, bartenders, and security people all usually will have some kind of standard agreement form which stipulates what the couple gets, when, and how much it costs.

It's a good idea to take contracts home to read before putting pen to paper and writing a deposit check. Even a seemingly easy-to-understand contract may leave out important details which need to be covered. Besides, who can concentrate when a busy salesperson hovers close by, anxious to close a deal?

Read everything carefully. If there are items you don't like, make a copy of the contract and circle the items to discuss with the provider. You may be surprised at the flexibility inherent in any contract. Like prices, they're not always non-negotiable. If you find the agreement leaves out important details, feel free to add a sentence or two on the copy of the contract to cover them. In short, amend the contract to suit you.

Here are just some details to look for. It's by no means a complete list.

Catering

Delivery times for food, what kinds of food along with quantities, who will serve it and clean up, and what happens to leftovers; will the provider include containers. Extra charges. When balance is due.

Photographers

Photo shoot sites: bride's home, ceremony, reception, and how much for each. Who's authorized to direct the photographer to take pictures (everyone will ask him or her, so provide for this in advance). Any overtime pay for photographers. Film development costs and delivery date. Size and type of prints. Album. Video. Charges for editing. Will negatives be stored and for how long?

Reception halls

Date and time, cost, decorations, setup, cleanup, overtime costs if reception goes longer than planned.

Flowers

The types of flowers expected and the fee. Will they deliver? Delivery time and fee. Floral arrangement costs. Accessories provided.

Gowns

Type, color, fabrics, and manufacturer of gown and/or bridesmaids dresses. Pickup times for gowns and what happens if you don't pick them up at the specified time.

Watch the details and work together with the provider to make the agreement as comprehensive as is sensible to both parties. Most providers should appreciate your attention to details. They dislike problems as much as you do, and they understand the importance of written agreements in terms of how they can help assure that all goes as smoothly as planned.

When both parties agree to the amended contract, if amendments are required, both should initial changes, sign, and date the document. Both should retain a copy.

It's a good idea to keep all such information in one place. Pendaflex files or loose-leaf notebooks with holders are handy organizational tools. In fact, it's smart to keep all information gathered from the outset in a notebook. You'll avoid wondering where a vital estimate or other documentation has gone and going crazy trying to find it.

Before signing the contract, make sure you have checked the provider's references. Ask for the names of some recent customers and call them for an evaluation of the provider's performance. In addition, make certain to actually see the documentation required of providers requiring licenses and insurance. For example, does the limo service have all necessary state and local licenses and insurance? Does the band or DJ or the caterer have insurance?

After the contract is signed, it will be too late to ask questions aimed at finding out whether the provider is all he or she is cracked up to be. All wedding experts stress checking references and getting the details, even the little ones such as the names of musicians hired to play in the band you selected, listed in the contract. With so much money on the line, not to mention the quality of your celebration, it pays to be cautious and thorough.

CHAPTER
9

Bridal Shows

Attending a bridal show is a lot of fun and a great source of information for brides, mothers of the bride, and grooms, too. These shows are based on the trade show concept common in most every major industry. Vendors and manufacturers within a given industry come together in one place to show off the latest services and products for distributors, retailers, and end-users.

As you will see, the wedding industry is just like others. Trade shows play a big part of it. There is a distinction, however, between a pure trade show, which has a business-to-business slant, and a bridal show aimed at the end-user who happens to be the bride, groom, a family member, or friend involved in the wedding or honeymoon. But the concept of bringing the major players together in one place to promote and transact business is the same.

The bridal show is of value to couples planning a wedding for many reasons. Attending one will give the couple a crash course in the wedding planning process. Try to attend one early on.

This will allow you to gather as much information as possible, get a bead on prices, and to see with your own eyes the various products available—from invitations to gowns.

Also, what you learn at the bridal show will help you be a better shopper when using the phone book, answering ads in bridal magazines and newspaper wedding sections, and when contacting referrals.

Typically, vendors at bridal shows will include bridal shops, gown manufacturers, photographers, DJs and bands, limousine services, cosmetic and hair style specialists, florists, reception hall and hotel representatives, and many others. Honeymoon consultants, real estate agents, and insurance agents also attend these shows.

For the vendors, the shows bring together a ready market with cash to burn. It's a little like shooting fish in a barrel for them. The prospects are packed together and eager listeners to sales pitches.

A bridal show usually isn't complete without a fashion show. This is an exciting moment for the bride-to-be because it gives her a chance to visualize herself in all the glorious gowns, along with every conceivable accessory right down to the shoes. Lingerie, evening wear, groom's attire, and casual honeymoon attire also may figure into the fashion show.

In addition to the fashion show, a DJ and band showcase is usually part of a bridal show. Various DJs and bands will play for about twenty minutes each. This lets you hear the acts and see their live "stage presence."

Bridal show promoters say the one-stop shopping approach saves dozens of hours in the wedding and honeymoon planning process. This is true, if you go to a bridal show as if you were shopping at a supermarket, simply pulling what strikes your fancy off the shelves and plunking the merchandise into a cart.

The convenience holds a great appeal to busy couples. It's very tempting to fall into the one-stop shopping trap. To add to your temptation, vendors offer nice, juicy show discounts. These may seem great while in the exciting atmosphere with all those other future brides and grooms. When door prizes are given out, the feel to these shows can border on electric. Love is in the air and the cash registers are jingling happily away.

Be wary of the great deals, though. Good transactions can be made at shows, saving lots of money. But if you haven't already done your homework on average prices in your market for various services and products, you could wind up signing on for what you thought was a good deal only to find out later you got caught in the mark-up game.

Any astute shopper knows that stores mark up products, then advertise a "sale." Twenty percent off a product marked up 30 percent isn't a bargain. That's not to say this goes on all the time at bridal shows, just that the overhead of attending the show must be made up by the providers, and they're not likely to eat the costs...not when they can pass them on to you.

The cheapskate approach to bridal shows employs two tactics:

1. Go to a show or two very early in the planning stage and use it as an informational source to learn about the wedding and honeymoon planning process and to identify providers you might want to deal with. If you find providers you think you like, ask them if they will be present at other shows in the near future; they probably will be.

Also, tell them you may be interested in signing up for their services but still haven't made up your mind. Ask about their availability on the date you plan to get married and if they can accommodate your requirements.

This will invite some pressure from them to have you sign up right away to be sure they can accommodate you. They may well not have an opening if you wait, but remember that's part of the game. They want you to commit; if you don't get them, it won't be the end of the world, so don't get pressured into a contract signing unless you're really sure about it.

2. Next, go out and explore the market to verify whether those great show discounts really were as good as they sounded. After that process has been completed, if you still want to deal with a provider you found at a show call to see if they'll give you the show discount, since that's where you found them. They may say the discount only applies to contracts signed at shows, but if they're really interested in your business they may waive that requirement.

Try calling for the discount first. If it fails, go to another show you know the provider will attend and sign up at the show discount price.

Employing the cheapskate approach will enable you to get the biggest bang for your buck and avoid traps which less astute shoppers will fall into. It'll take more time and labor, but you'll find it's worth it.

Most major metropolitan and suburban areas have loads of bridal shows. You can find out about them through wedding ad sections in large newspapers, bridal magazines in some cases, regional bridal guides, and local bridal shops. Find out where shows in your area are held and call for more information.

CHAPTER
10

Invitations and More

The price of wedding invitations and announcements in traditional formats has been increasing dramatically in the 1990s, largely due to rapid increases in the cost of paper. Yet despite price hikes, a professionally printed traditional invitation and wedding announcement package is still reasonable. (Wedding announcements are sent out the day of your wedding to family, friends, and coworkers not invited to the celebration.)

According to reports from leading manufacturers of thermographic wedding stationery, the average price for invitations and announcements is $340. That's an average. Less expensive options can cut that figure by more than half.

Stationery packages range from simple to complex and are priced accordingly. The more design elements included, such as four-color art, foil, ribbons, lace and other frills, the more the package will cost. Simpler stationery, fewer add-ons, and creative approaches which cost less money are the way to go for the cheapskate approach.

There are three basic types of printing processes that can be used to produce the stationery packages: engraving, thermography, and offset printing.

At one time, engraving was the only accepted reproduction

method. It uses a copper plate which provides the sharpest, cleanest raised letters possible. The wealthy still use engraving, but overall sales are declining. The low end price for a complete, simple invitation package which includes thank-you notes, starts at around $500.

Thermography uses a much less expensive paper plate. Talcum powder is sprinkled on the ink before it dries to create the raised lettering. The images don't look as sharp as engraved images, but they are still good quality. Thermography is the most popular production method.

Offset printing requires an inexpensive paper plate as well. However, it doesn't produce the raised lettering so many couples prefer. It's also not used very often because it's more expensive than using a large company specializing in thermography.

Where to Start

Local bridal shops, print shops, and other sources offer invitations and announcements. These providers serve as dealers for large companies which produce the materials. The dealers get a cut of the action from the large companies. Prices you see in the sample books are retail; the dealer's cut is hidden.

You can eliminate the middle man by scanning the ads in your favorite bridal magazines for companies advertising invitations and announcements. These firms will sell to you directly through mail order, saving you money and providing the convenience of home shopping. Officials from large commercial invitation companies say an increasing number of couples are going the direct mail-order route, though they still report brisk sales of their products sold through dealers.

Contact the mail-order company and request a catalog. It will include samples of invitation packages and all the other information you need to make up your mind. For your convenience, some mail-order companies which may give you better prices than those available through dealers are listed at the end of this chapter.

Commercial dealers such as print shops will have a variety of sample books to look through. These will include a wide range of wedding accessories from personalized matchbooks and napkins to toasting goblets. They are a great one-stop shopping source. Even if you plan to order from a direct mail catalog, take a look at what your local businesses offer and compare prices before ordering.

Order slightly more materials than you think you'll need. Most manufacturers consider reorders as new. In other words, you won't get a price break simply because you already placed an order. This is due to the costs of press setup and cleanup, and other factors.

Order your invitation and thank-you stationery as soon as possible. Four or five months before the wedding date is a good bet. This will allow time for printing and correcting errors, and time to address the envelopes for the invitations and thank-you notes at the same time.

Ordering early will avoid extra charges for advance ship-ment of envelopes from commercial printers. Many couples are in a rush and have to pay $10 to $15 in surcharges, plus additional shipping costs for advance receipt of envelopes. This isn't the cheapskate approach. It's silly to duplicate shipping costs and to pay a surcharge when you don't have to. Order the whole package early, so you can get going on addressing the envelopes.

Mail your invitations six to eight weeks ahead of the wedding date.

Go with simple thermographic invitation packages with flat-card or inexpensive folded formats and use black ink. Color inks cost extra. Avoid the extras no matter how tempt-ing they are as you go through the sample books. Or, try other options listed later in this chapter.

Despite the fact that more couples are paying the expenses for their weddings, the tradition naming the bride's parents as hosts of the reception party still holds. The invitation package customarily goes out under their names.

Some couples, however, elect to send the invitations out under their own names. That's okay, too. Do what's comfortable for everyone involved.

What's in the Invitation Package

The traditional formal wedding invitation ensemble includes the following components:

- Inner ungummed envelope to house the inserts, plus tissue (once used to guard against ink smudges)
- Outer gummed envelope for mailing
- Adhesive envelope seal (once done with wax)
- Response (R.S.V.P.) card and envelope
- Reception card (for guests invited to both the ceremony and the reception, and if your reception will be held at a different location than the ceremony)
- New address (At-Home) cards to tell guests where the couple will be living
- Church pew cards for special seating arrangements (for very formal weddings with guests of honor, definitely not needed for the cheapskate approach)
- Personalized thank-you notes and envelopes

As you can see, all of these pieces of the puzzle can ring up quite a fat bill. You may not need to go with all the traditional components, but they are listed to guide you through your decision-making process.

Cost Savings on the Standard Package

Prices vary from company to company and state to state. However, the playing field of major firms specializing in wedding stationery thermography continues to dwindle, leaving only the big guys. These national firms all know each other's rates and price themselves according to what the market will bear.

The prices below are based on averages taken from the larger commercial companies in today's market on the most basic invitation packages available through dealers; mail order will be less, though not a lot less. Prices are based on one hundred invitations printed with black ink and no four-color decorative designs.

1. Go without fancy envelope liners and seals. Don't use foil or color inks and don't add anything to the standard wording listed in the sample book. Some dealers charge around $20 for envelope liners and around $15 for seals on orders of one hundred envelopes.
   Your savings: $35.
2. You can eliminate the new address card (At-Home card). Consider these two suggestions:
   • When you send your thank you note, mention your new address in the text or ask that recipients take note of your new return address on the mailing envelope.
   • Make your own new address card on your personal computer and include it as an insert in your thank-you note. You'll save between $25 and $35 dollars on an order of one hundred—more if you've chosen a fancy format.
3. If all the guests will be attending your ceremony and reception, and both will be held at the same site, the words "Reception to immediately follow" on the invitation will be sufficient. If the reception will be held at a different location, give the address and the time.

Many companies give you four lines of copy on the invitation free of charge. Industry officials say approximately 85 percent of the customers use it for reception information instead of paying for a separate reception card, despite the etiquette which says this is a no no.

This will eliminate the reception card. Your savings on one hundred cards equals $35 or more.

Some purists say the use of footnotes or including reception information on the invitation is socially incorrect. It's up to you to decide how much a slave you want to be to wedding etiquette.

4. Instead of a response card, you can simply put R.S.V.P. or Please Respond with the date you want your reply on the bottom of the invitation.

Response cards with envelopes can be costly. Total base cost for one hundred response cards and envelopes with a return address printing charge starts at roughly $60.

Your savings: $60

5. You can buy preprinted thank-you notes from stationers with Thank You on the cover and no text inside, as opposed to personalized stationery.

Some companies have preprinted thank-you notes inside their covers, but this is one area where you don't want to take the easy way out. Get preprinted stationery for your thank-you note covers, but you need to write your thanks yourself. Make sure they're blank inside.

Price the preprinted thank-you notes against the prices for personalized thank-you notes available through the big printing companies either direct to you or through a middleman. In some cases, with the high price of paper these days, the price difference will be minimal and you'll be better off paying for nicer personalized thank-you notes.

Another option is to order personalized thank-you notes, but not envelopes with return addresses printed on them. Return address printing is a nice add-on for the companies. It's tacky to order formal invitations, reception cards, and announcements, then stick adhesive address labels (ordered from major catalog companies) on the envelopes. But it's far more acceptable to do so with your thank-you notes since they're informal communications between you and your guests.

You can order one hundred sheets of personalized thank-you notes and envelopes without return addresses printed on them for as little as $35.

The typical charge for printing a return address is roughly $30 for the first one hundred envelopes. Why not save that money and use adhesive labels? If you think even nice adhesive labels are tacky, why not handwrite all the return addresses, including those on the invitations? Handwriting return addresses on the invitation, response card envelope, and the thank-you note will save $90 or more. Add savings for announcement envelopes as well.

TOTAL MINIMAL SAVINGS WITH THE CHEAPSKATE APPROACH: $185

ROUGH ESTIMATE FOR REMAINDER OF PACKAGE FOR ONE HUNDRED GUESTS: $100

The package would include one hundred inner and outer envelopes with tissue and return address printed, the invitation in black ink, and one hundred sheets of personalized thank-you stationery and envelopes with no return address printed.

If you go with a reception card, add an additional $35 or so.

If you must go with a response card and envelopes, add an additional minimum of $40.

This brings your price up to around $175. Add another $64 for postage at 1996 rates if you're including stamped response cards and your invitation package weighs less than one ounce.

Order a sample package of your invitation stationery and weigh it at the post office before mailing in your order, so you'll know up front if it's going to exceed one ounce and almost double your postal rate (you may want to choose another invitation package). It'll also save you delays, which sometimes can be disastrous, when invitations are returned due to insufficient postage.

And about those return addresses on the back flap of the mailing envelope you sometimes see—they're big trouble. Postal regulations require return address placement on the upper left top corner in the front of the envelope. Write your return address on the back flap and you might not get the letter returned if the postman decides he's had enough with dogs and bad weather and routes your misdirected invitation to the dead letter heap.

Even with cutting all the corners possible with the traditional invitation format from commercial dealers, you'll still be hard pressed to get away with spending less than $160 for the package and postage, or slightly less with direct mail companies. Still, that's not too bad at only 1.6 percent of a total hypothetical budget of $10,000.

Create Your Own Invitation on Your Personal Computer

If you're not afraid to drop tradition and all the etiquette accompanying it, you'll save a bundle. This will be easier if you're having a small or informal wedding, increasingly difficult if you're going the formal route. But it's something to think about.

You can create your own invitation on your personal computer for next to nothing. The invitation can include a favorite poem, song lyrics, and all the information your guests need in one format (reception and R.S.V.P.). Best of all, it can be fun and creative and sent in one outer envelope with a nice adhesive return address label.

You'll need good computer software capable of changing the size of letters and the style, and a letter-quality or laser printer. Make a master layout and take it to your local printer for photocopying on good paper with 25 percent rag; all-cotton papers cost a fortune. You'll want the heaviest paper you can get through the photocopier, not a standard twenty-five pound weight. Talk with your printer and ask to see paper samples.

Using this method, you could get away with simple invitations that cost less than a dime each for photocopying or about $10 for one hundred (or only $5 if the layout included two invitations on one 8½ by 11-inch sheet). Add another $10 for envelopes and $32 for first-class postage. The total comes to a whopping $31 to $52 for the invitation package.

Producing your own package on your computer no doubt will give some purists a coronary. Utter sacrilege, they'll scream. But who cares what they think! If you're having an informal or semi-formal wedding and aren't "married" to tradition, go for what makes you happy. With a good computer software package, a letter-quality or laser printer, and a little creativity, you can create some very nice invitations yourself.

Pre-printed, Fill-in-the-Blank Packages

Major companies such as Hallmark produce value packs of invitations which come with mailing envelopes. The traditional wording format in raised or flat letters appears on the cards. Blanks are left for the personalized information such as names, dates, and places.

For a couple planning a small, informal or semi-formal wedding (particularly if it does not include an evening reception), preprinted invitations as well as wedding announcements can mean substantial savings. They're a great alternative for a bride who's good at calligraphy or has reasonably good handwriting (or knows someone who can help).

One hundred Hallmark preprinted invitations and envelopes cost approximately $30. Reception card packages cost about the same. So do those for wedding announcements.

The envelopes won't have return addresses printed on them. Use nice adhesive labels or write by hand. For around $60, plus $32 for postage, you can send out your invitations and reception cards.

You may want to include a return postcard for R.S.V.P. responses. You can get blank postcards with the postage printed on them for twenty cents from your post office; paper is free.

An oversized three-line ink stamp for under $10, available through catalog companies, will let you print the few lines needed on your response cards. When ordering, you should be able to open enough space between the lines to allow room for the respondent to write.

> *Example:* The favor of a reply is requested by (date)
> Name _____
> Number of persons _____

Adding the $20 for response postcards and $10 for the ink stamp, the total price of the invitation packages is roughly $122.

This is also a great way to go if you're producing your own invitations on your personal computer and want to include a response card with the package. Why pay for one hundred extra envelopes plus first-class postage when a simple postcard response will do just fine?

Handwritten, Casual

For couples planning a small informal or semi-formal wedding with around fifty to seventy-five guests, handwriting the invitations on plain old nice stationery is perfectly acceptable. Include reception information and R.S.V.P. or response postcards.

All-cotton stationery with matching envelopes could run around $50 or more, depending on paper size, any frills such as borders, and the individual retailer price. Buy less expensive wood pulp stationery; it's still very nice and nobody will particularly care if you don't use an all-cotton brand. Why pay more?

Names and Numbers

Your Cost-Saving Adhesive Labels

Many catalog companies offer personalized adhesive return address labels. Current, Inc., based in Colorado Springs, Colorado, is a very good source. Among others, they offer "clear" labels which don't look like an adhesive label. You can still tell it's a label, but it's not as distracting or clunky looking. At 1996 rates, you can order a roll of six hundred labels for $6.95.

To order a catalog or to place an order call Current, Inc. at (800) 848-2848. Allow five to eight days to receive the catalog, and three to four weeks to receive your labels…a little longer during Christmas rush times.

Mail-order Invitation Companies

The American Wedding: (800) 428-0379

Wedding Invitations by Romantic Moments: (800) 826-2704

Now & Forever Wedding Stationery: (800) 451-8616

Wedding Invitations by Wedding Treasures: (800) 851-5974

Heritage Weddings (African-American invitations and wedding accessories): (800) 892-4291

Evangel Wedding (Christian invitations and wedding accessories): (800) 342-4227

CHAPTER
11

The All-Important Gown

A bride dressed in a beautiful gown as she walks down the aisle to take her vows is something very special indeed. The effect touches all who see her, especially the groom. Romance fills the air and joy fills the hearts of all present to witness the wedding ceremony, for a bride and groom's marriage is one of the few rites of passage between two people celebrated universally in every country on the globe.

When people think of brides today they immediately envision a beautiful woman dressed in a white or ivory colored gown. This is in keeping with the custom which began in the late 1700s and came of age in Victorian times. The vast majority of gowns sold in the United States today are white.

Back in the 1800s, fancy white gowns were mostly purchased for the weddings of well-heeled urbanites in the East. Out west, brides from hard-working families seldom wore white, favoring their Sunday best or borrowing the prettiest dress available from another woman in the town. If it happened to be white, so much the better. Few could afford gowns ordered from bridal shops in cities such as Boston and New York.

White has symbolized purity and innocence since the

Greeks endowed the color with those ethereal properties, and it still holds true. Conversely, black and red have long been associated with evil, at least in Western cultures. (However, Chinese brides in traditional ceremonies always wear red). Yet blue, a symbol of true love, and pink, the essence of femininity, have traditionally been acceptable colors, and at informal weddings they still are. Champagne-colored gowns are also worn.

Green, yellow, gray, and brown are not usually associated with wedding gowns. These colors all carry with them a load of superstitions as unpleasant as those for black and red. However, it's interesting to note that bridesmaids aren't saddled with the same limitations, with the possible exception of the rather somber gray which is more suitable for funerals than weddings.

For the bride, selecting a gown and the accessories to go with it is one of the most exciting parts of planning a wedding, but it can also be very confusing. The dress she wears reflects who she is and how she likes to be perceived. The gown makes a statement as unique as the individual bride, and designers worldwide offer plenty of styles to choose from. They know brides come in all shapes and sizes, have varied budgets, and want different things when looking for a gown.

The average gown, if there is such a thing, costs around $700. But according to bridal magazines and some wedding consultants, the typical bride will spend between $1,000 and $2,000 for her dress and accessories. The prices vary among bridal gown designers for many reasons, not the least of which are the types of fabrics used, how the gown is produced, and the complexity of the design.

Just like virtually every other aspect of the wedding planning process, selecting a gown isn't simple. It's easy to get caught up in the emotion of the moment and fall in love with a gown that'll break the bank. Many brides wish they could ask an expert questions before entering a sales situation where there is pressure, either obvious or subtle, to buy.

ASK PRISCILLA OF BOSTON

Patricia Kaneb, president and chief executive officer of
Priscilla of Boston, offers tips on how to select a gown and
how to do it without spending more than the budget allows.
While some of you might associate Priscilla of Boston with
very upscale, expensive gowns, the bulk of her gowns sell for
between $1,000 and $2,000 in the more than two hundred
stores nationwide which carry them. This fifty-year-old
company has long set the standards in the industry. If there's
one thing Patricia knows, it's gowns!

Q.   My future husband doesn't understand why my gown is
so important to me. Can you explain it to him?

A.   In the fifties and sixties there were a lot more formal
events such as balls and dinner parties where women had a
chance to wear very formal dresses. Today the wedding is one
of the few times where she's the center of attention wearing a
formal gown.

Her wedding is one of the few days in her life where she'll
have all eyes on her while she's wearing a very feminine dress,
and she wants to look her very best. She may not ever have
the opportunity to wear a dress constructed in the same way
again (custom-made or tailor-fitted to her figure).

The gown makes her feel beautiful on her wedding day. It's
important to understand that, and to let her feel special.

Q.   What's the best way to get started looking for a gown
that's right for me?

A.   Educate yourself ahead of time by looking through
bridal magazines to find styles of gowns you like and want to
try on. Typically, the ads in the magazines will tell you which
stores carry the gown. It's better to find a store which carries
the styles you like rather than going from store to store with
no ideas.

Q.   How long does it usually take for brides to decide on a
particular dress?

A. That depends on how good an idea the bride has at the outset on what she wants. Usually brides visit a bridal shop at least two or three times before deciding to buy.

Q. I want to get the most attention I can from the bridal consultant at my local bridal shop. What's the best time to go?

A. If you're like most brides, you work a full-time job. That means weekends are very busy times at bridal shops, as are evenings, because all the other brides in your area are also looking after work. Appointments are harder to get in a hurry and the staff will have less time to spend with you than if you visit the shop during the week. I know it's tough to take time off from work for this, but if you'd like the most attention, weekday shopping is best.

Also, the first time you go to the store, don't bring a carload of your friends with you. One other person whose opinion you care about is good. The more people present, the longer the process will take, and that's not what you want.

Q. How far in advance of the wedding should I start looking?

A. The time frame from ordering to delivery and final fit is often lengthy because it's hard for the bride to schedule times for fittings. Also, when demand is high during peak ordering times, some companies get backlogged with orders.

Most stores quote four- to six-month time frames for making dresses individually. At our company, we make the dresses individually by hand here in Massachusetts and can deliver them more quickly than that if necessary.

Of course, if you buy a ready-to-wear dress or a sample, all you have to worry about are alterations and possibly a cleaning of the sample.

Q. How do I choose a bridal shop? There are so many around, how do I know which are good and which may not be the best for me?

A. Referrals are best. Speak to people you know who were recently married and bought their gown at the shop. The longevity of the store is important. If it's been around for many years serving generations of brides, it's obviously done something right.

Also. you want to find a store which does the alterations on the premises. It's more convenient for you, and it also means the store will have an incentive to make or deal with a quality product because they're responsible for the end result.

It's common to charge for alterations because they are expensive for the store to make. Be wary of stores which claim to give free alterations. They're making up the expense somewhere else.

One final point: if you're on a limited budget, select a gown which fits you well to start with, one which needs very few alterations. Most of the time, a few alterations are necessary, but some brides fall in love with a dress that will need lots of work to make it fit properly, and that's going to cost a lot of money. It's better to try another equally pretty gown that won't need lots of work to get the right fit.

Q. Is a big bridal shop better than a small one, or is the opposite true?

A. That's an individual choice. In my opinion, the smaller shops with a long-standing reputation for quality service and products are the best bet, but they will also be more expensive for obvious reasons. A big store with lots of capital can afford to sell at below suggested retail prices whereas the smaller stores can't cut their markups and stay in business very long.

It really depends on what you want. If you're shopping just on price, you should go to the larger stores, if there are any in your area. But there's nothing like the service from a seasoned professional who'll give you personal attention and stand behind products and services you're buying.

Q. Are there any advantages to the larger stores besides better prices?

A. Yes. The larger stores will often have more merchandise out on the floor for you to look at and try on. Many smaller stores have closed stock rooms, so all the dresses aren't on the floor. You'll be shown samples in styles by designers you like, but you won't see everything that's available.

You should decide if you want to see everything yourself on the sales floor or rely on consultants from the store to show you gowns in your preferred style and price range.

Q. Are bridal consultants at the stores important?

A. We believe relying on the consultant is a good way to go rather than going it alone or relying on advice from a friend or relative who may not have the expertise to be of the most help. The store consultant can judge colors and styles which will be flattering to you, and they're specialists who can help you find the best gown for you at a price you can afford.

Q. Can I buy a quality gown on a very limited budget? I've seen lots of beautiful gowns, but I can't afford $1,500 to $2,000.

A. The short answer to that question is yes. But it does get a little more complicated when you go into detail.

One great way to save as much as 40 to 50 percent off the retail price of a gown is to buy samples which have been discontinued or retired. Samples, of course, have been tried on before, but they can be in great condition, especially if the dress wasn't that popular.

Many stores will have samples at discounted prices. If you're on a very limited budget but still want a beautiful gown made from expensive natural fabrics, for example, don't be afraid to ask about these opportunities.

Often, all the sample dress needs is a good cleaning by a specialist to bring it back to mint condition. It's not inferior just because someone else tried it on. Ask the shop for a referral to a dry cleaner who specializes in gowns. On the high end, the fee for cleaning runs around $200.

Q. What if the bridal shop doesn't have any samples I like? Are there other ways to reduce the cost of my gown?

A. Gowns made overseas are generally a lot less expensive than those made in the United States. For one thing, labor costs are lower abroad. Many of the top designers take advantage of this to lower their retail prices.

There is a question of quality, though. The gowns made overseas are often done as piece work by a number of different people. The quality of the work is harder to control and may not be as good as that done by one person.

Q. Is the type of fabric an important factor in the cost for my gown? I just love silk, but I've heard it's really expensive.

A. You're right, silk certainly is expensive. Apart from how the dress is made, the fabric used is the most critical factor in the final cost. An average gown with a long train requires ten yards of fabric.

When it comes to retail prices for synthetic versus natural fabrics, natural fabrics such as silks range from $40 to $60 a yard. Synthetics can be priced as low as $16 a yard. If you want to save money, you may want to look at synthetic dresses. Some of them are well made and you can't tell the difference between the synthetic and natural fabrics unless you're an expert.

In the past, natural fabrics were almost exclusively used to produce gowns. That's not as true today. Synthetic fabrics are often used.

In fact, some of our best-selling gowns in the lower price range are made from synthetic fabrics. It's okay to buy gowns made from synthetic fabrics; times change and so do expectations. Just look for quality workmanship; poor quality can cause big trouble.

Q. I'm no expert, so how do I recognize quality?

A. You should look on the inside of the dress to see how well it's constructed. You can tell if it's been sloppily made. For example, if you're looking at a beaded dress, ask if all the beads are individually knotted or if the beads are on a string.

I've heard horror stories where the bride has gotten one of the beads stuck on something and the entire string of beads unraveled as she walked down the aisle. If beads are on a single thread, a single break can cause the whole thing to unravel at the worst time.

Also, choose a brand name that's well known. And go to a reputable shop.

Q. I love lace and want lots of it. Is that going to drive the price of the gown up?

A. It could, depending on where the lace is made. Domestic versus imported laces are another area where prices can vary greatly and affect the overall cost of the gown.

For example, we pay in some cases $150 per yard wholesale for imported French laces. But a lot of manufacturers are making knockoffs of imported French laces which cost as little as $30 per yard wholesale. You should ask about whether the lace is imported or domestic, and to see gowns only with domestic lace if you're trying to save money.

Q. What's the most important thing I should consider besides price, the style of the dress, the designer, and the shop when looking for a gown?

A. I think it's very important for you to realize that regardless of the price of the dress, if it fits well, it's going to look nice. The fit is the most important factor. You can buy good quality, lower-priced gowns that fit well and look smashing. An expensive gown is nice, of course, but just because you can't afford one doesn't mean you have to settle on a gown which doesn't make you look great. You want to feel comfortable and relaxed wearing your gown.

Remember, there are lots of gowns out there from which you can choose. You'll find one you love, and you're going to look fantastic wearing it!

Making Your Own Gown

It's not done often, but some brides do save money by making their own gowns or by having a friend or relative who's a good seamstress make one as a wedding gift. The make-it-yourself tactic can enable you to get a gown made from natural fabrics versus synthetics, bringing these more expensive materials in line with your budget.

The price for an average of ten yards or so of good quality natural fabrics runs around $500 to $600. The lace and beading will be extra and prices vary widely.

If you want to really cut costs, which makes sense if you're spending all that time on labor, try a synthetic known as poly-organza fabric. It's a milky colored sheer fabric which costs as little as $6 a yard retail. That's only around $60 to $70 for fabric, versus $500 to $600. Some of the best designers and manufacturers use it, including Priscilla of Boston. It's mostly used for gowns worn at spring and summer weddings.

If you're in an urban area or close to a big city, shop for your fabric in the garment district where you can buy directly from a wholesaler. You'll save even more money.

"The Second Time Around"

Some brides wear their mother's gowns, though this isn't done as often as it once was. Or they borrow a gown from a friend or relative who was recently married. The only hitch here is alteration costs. Remember, the fit is all-important and alterations are expensive.

Depending on where you live, you may find some stores offer gown resales. These aren't usually bridal shops, but stores which take all sorts of clothes on consignment. A resale made from natural fabrics can cost as little as $300, though they often are more expensive than that. A resale could be the way to get that super costly gown which might otherwise be out of reach.

Some brides having informal weddings don't buy traditional gowns at all. They order a bridesmaids gown in white instead. This type of gown can be worn again as an evening dress at other formal occasions, which will also save you money.

Some stores rent gowns, just like they rent tuxedos. The fee will be close to what you'd pay for a resale. But you can't have a rented gown altered to fit your figure, which is a big disadvantage. Bear in mind too that rentals and resales are more difficult to find.

To Keep the Gown or Not

Gown preservation can ring up added costs you don't need. In the past, the majority of brides kept their gowns. Today, many still do, but an increasing number take them to resale shops. The shop will sell the gown for you on consignment, taking a 50 percent cut on the price. Selling your gown may seem a bit mercenary, but it's a way to get back some dollars which would otherwise have sat in the attic along with hungry moths anxious to eat your dress.

You might buy a really expensive gown and justify the cost by saying your daughter will wear it someday. You might not want to sell it for this reason, too. But times have changed and most often the bride wants her own dress. Your daughter is likely to feel the same way.

Accessories

The price for headpieces often surprises brides. They figure the big bucks go for the gown, but a quality headpiece which matches the gown can cost a lot of money, too. At Priscilla of Boston, they make their own headpieces and match them to the gowns using the same laces and the same beading. The average price for a headpiece and veil runs from $300 to $400.

Headpieces bought off the rack which don't exactly match the gown, but still look nice, will greatly reduce the costs. Of course, the more elaborate designs cost more than simple ones.

Some brides prefer to wear a pretty bow or a simple wreath of flowers. This costs a lot less than a formal headpiece and a long veil.

When selecting a headpiece, be aware that it shouldn't "fight" with your gown. The two should work together to create the visual appeal you desire. If you have a simple gown, don't buy an elaborate headpiece. If you have an elaborate gown, you can still use a less elaborate headpiece but one that's overly simple will look out of place.

Footwear

Shoes come in price ranges so wide it's hard to pin down. Dyeable shoes are often purchased because they are relatively inexpensive and can be dyed to exactly match the color of your gown. Some stores will cover shoes with the fabric used to make your gown, but this is more costly than dye.

Consider plain white or off-white pumps instead of shoes gilded with all sorts of fancy decorations. The simple white leather pumps will still look elegant and you'll have the advantage of being able to wear them during the summer. Besides, how many people will be watching your feet? If you're wearing a miniskirt or ankle-length gown, you may want to get a little fancier, but save the money on shoes. They're not as important as your gown and headpiece.

Of course, you'll want jewelry to go with your gown, a nice handbag, and perhaps gloves. A good thing to keep in mind is that all the extras add up; don't go overboard. Also, when it comes to jewelry, some bridal magazines build in as much as $1,000 or more for it. You needn't spend that kind of money. Just keep it simple. Consider borrowing jewelry to keep costs down.

Your Bridesmaids

The gown you select will directly influence the types of gowns your bridesmaids wear. You won't be paying for their gowns, of course, but keep their budgets in mind when you select your wedding dress. If you know that the maid or matron of honor, your bridesmaids, and your flower girl (if you're having one) are on limited budgets, keep this in mind. Planning a simpler, less formal wedding, and selecting a simpler gown for yourself will reduce the financial burdens of those you love.

If you know your potential bridesmaids have already participated in other weddings, they may not be able to afford to be key players in yours. The financial situation of others should enter into your thinking.

When you've selected a bridal shop which has a gown you like, line up your maid or matron of honor and your bridesmaids to buy their gowns there. Work with the owner of the bridal shop on a discount for yourself and for them. The total amount of money spent for your gown, accessories, and for those of your female attendants will run several thousand dollars in many cases. That's a lot of buying power; use it to get a discount if one isn't offered to you without your asking.

The Groom's Tuxedo

Although some grooms are wearing double-breasted suits at more informal weddings today, the majority of grooms still wear tuxedos. This is in part because traditional weddings are by far the most common, and that means the bride wears a nice white wedding gown necessitating that her man wears a tux to go with it.

The majority of men will never wear a tuxedo except on rare occasions such as a prom or to their own wedding or if they've been asked to stand up at a friend's. So, 90 percent of the time, the guy rents a tuxedo. There is none of the pull to buy as there is with the bride.

A good tuxedo rental will run around $100 to $150. You can rent one for more or less, depending on where you live and where you shop. Like the bride's gown, your tuxedo must fit properly.

When you go to the tux shop, bring a photo of your bride's gown or at least a swatch of the fabric to show the store consultant. Tell him or her about the type of wedding you're planning, and listen to any advice you're given.

Your best man and groomsmen will be wearing the same style tuxedos at a formal wedding. It makes good sense to ask them to shop at the same store for two reasons: the clothes will match, and you can get a discount. Many stores offer grooms a free tuxedo with four or five male attendants. The money you save can go toward the gifts you'll buy for them.

Some bridal shops also rent tuxedos. If your bride's does, shop there because you'll increase your chances for a better discount.

CHAPTER
12

On Golden Chariots: Transportation

When planning the transportation of the bride and groom and their wedding party, the desire for the grand and glorious is natural. An ordinary car won't cut it. How about an Excalibur or a superstretch limousine to add even more magic to the ceremony and reception? Caught up in the moment, couples tend to go overboard and rent very expensive transportation.

It's okay to want the very best transportation. In fact, between 1982 and 1992 the number of couples hiring limousines for transportation on their wedding days increased by 55 percent, according to the National Limousine Association in Washington, D.C. Today, well in excess of 72 percent of couples hire limousines and the percentage is increasing, largely due to concerns about drinking and driving. Transportation for weddings makes up a significant share of the $5 billion in annual revenue spent for limousine service nationwide.

But like all other key players in the main budget categories, the transportation provider must be researched with care. Prices vary widely and it's easy to pay too much.

The following are some tips from Wayne Smith, executive director of the National Limousine Association, on how to hire limousine companies without going broke.

HIRING LIMOUSINE COMPANIES

Q. Is it true that most limousine companies structure their rates per vehicle hired for a wedding based on a national average of $50 per hour?

A. Yes, that's true. Your package may be marketed as a flat rate per vehicle, but the price should be broken out into a fee totaling around $50 per hour per vehicle. If it's higher, you're paying too much. Four hours is the typical time alloted for packages and a mandatory 15 percent gratuity is charged in addition to the base price.

If you go over the four-hour limit, an overtime charge of $50 per hour is common. Some companies put a premium on overtime, charging as much as $50 per half hour on overtime rates. If you think you're going to need more time than alloted in the package, negotiate for that in your contract.

Q. I've called around to lots of companies in my area and I've found many companies are more expensive than $50 per hour. Why is that?

A. A limousine company which caters mostly to corporate customers and has very few white stretch bridal limousines will tend to charge a lot more for wedding services. Demand for the bridal limousines might be high due to limited competition; or, if the company doesn't do a lot of wedding business, the owner will want to get as much profit from the cars when he or she can.

A limousine company specializing in weddings will have lots of bridal limousines in the fleet and will want to keep them on the road as much as possible. This is the kind of company which will give you the best price.

Q. How do I know if the company has a big fleet of
wedding limousines? I've called companies advertising
wedding services in regional wedding guides and found their
prices were very high. Wouldn't a company advertising in a
wedding publication have a big fleet of bridal limousines?

A. Not necessarily. In fact, the opposite might be the case.
A primarily corporate company with only a few limousines
for weddings would naturally want to generate business for
that area of the operation. Placing an ad in wedding
publications would help.

The only way to really determine the balance between the
number of corporate limousines and bridal limousines in a
company's fleet is to go see the fleet in person. You can ask
over the phone, but that's not the best way to go.

Q. Is it common for couples planning to hire a limousine
service for their wedding to go see the fleet? Doesn't that take
lots of time?

A. More couples should go see the cars and negotiate the
contract with the owner of the limousine company in person.
Unfortunately, many order the service right from the phone
book. It's not like calling a taxi. It might take time to do the
legwork, but it's worth the effort.

You can often negotiate a better price if you deal with the
owner. You can specify a particular car in your contract,
which will guarantee that's the one you get on your wedding
day or you'll pay less in the event another one is used. You can
see the condition of the cars, how the drivers are dressed, and
get a feel for the company you can't get on the phone.

Q. You keep mentioning contracts. Is a contract really that
important?

A. Contracts are very important. The horror stories I've
heard all arise from misunderstandings between both parties.
It becomes a"he said, she said" situation, and when nothing is
in writing, you can't tell what was promised and the company
won't know what you expect to receive for your money.

Specify such things as dates, times and places for pickups and dropoffs, wait times, time frames and fees, the driver's attire, the amount of gratuity, the specific car, and the company's travel range which doesn't cost extra. All these details are important.

Q. Should I really ask to see the owner's credentials? Won't that be a little insulting, as if I don't trust the owner?

A. Reputable companies should show you their credentials without your asking. If the owner doesn't offer, ask to see his or her state and local licenses and proof of insurance.

Q. Can you offer any tips on saving money?

A. In parts of the country where there is a peak wedding season, demand for limousine services during those periods will be very high. Prices will also be high. Think about having your wedding at off-peak times because prices will be lower.

Most people get married on Saturdays. This is also a high price time. Getting married during the week can save you between 10 and 20 percent on limousine fees. Rates for morning weddings are also less.

If you're not having an elaborate wedding, consider hiring a chauffeured luxury sedan. These cost around $35 per hour as opposed to $50 for a limousine.

Q. Is it true that a silver or black limousine costs less?

A. Yes. These cars are also used for corporate services, so the company has lots of opportunities to earn a profit from the cars. Demand for silver and black limousines is lower for weddings than the white bridal limousines. As a consequence, they are priced around 10 percent less on average.

Q. If a limousine company offers red-carpet treatment and free champagne for the bride and groom, does that mean the company will be more expensive to cover the extra costs?

A. Not at all. The limousine companies that do a big wedding business often include these services at no extra charge.

Other Money-Saving Ideas

Aside from the safety reasons for hiring limousines to avoid drinking and driving among the wedding party, the avoidance of crumpled gowns also bears consideration. A limousine will provide plenty of room for the bride's gown, and for those of her bridesmaids.

When the bride chooses her gown, it will also influence the type and size of her bridesmaids' gowns. Choosing a large, flowing gown will push you toward having to rent a limousine, and one or two more for the bridesmaids and groomsmen, plus the families of the bride and groom. Most brides don't think of that when they're shopping for their gowns, but it does bear some thought.

Another thought worth considering is the advantage of having your ceremony and reception at the same location. This will eliminate the trip from the ceremony site to the reception site, allowing you to negotiate a package based on the shorter number of hours needed to transport the bride from her home to the ceremony.

If you're having the ceremony and reception at different locations, try to have them both a short distance apart. This will save you money in potential overtime charges.

If you plan to head off to the airport directly after the reception, and you want limousine service, enter into a separate contract for that service. This way you won't have a limousine and driver waiting around while you celebrate. Consider a cab to the airport; it's cheaper.

Apart from negotiating directly with the owner of the limousine company for a special discount offered only to you, check out regional bridal guides or newspaper wedding sections for ads offering percentage or price discounts. Often, companies will offer these discounts as a way of tracking response to their advertising. Make sure you compare prices, though, since companies advertising in these publications may not necessarily be the best priced for your needs.

Consider the costs of three six-seater limousines for a four-hour package: minimum of $650, plus 15 percent gratuity of $97.50. Total: $747.50.

Compare that against the price for one chauffeured luxury sedan for the bride and groom: $140, plus 15 percent gratuity of $21. Total: $161.

Consider having the groomsmen chauffeur the bridesmaids in their own vehicles, and letting the families of the bride and groom drive their own cars as well. The bride's family traditionally pays for the transportation of the bridal party from the bride's home to the ceremony site, then to the reception. But today the couple often pays.

This is your special day, so by all means rent a luxury sedan or one limousine for a small bridal party. Limousines typically come in six, eight, and ten passenger sizes. But forget about the Rolls Royce. It may look wonderful and feel like a golden chariot, but the practical side of finances should win out. Spend the money you save on transportation elsewhere in the wedding budget or save it for the honeymoon!

Ceremonies and Receptions

The Ceremony

A church wedding. It's something most brides dream of, and most end up choosing. The choice is satisfying on many levels—religious, social, and economic. There often isn't a site fee for members of a church or synagogue, and the wedding ceremony costs are nominal at around $100 to $250 including donations and musician fees.

Of course a downside exists. A traditional church wedding costs more for flowers, limousine services, musicians, time, and convenience. The church wedding usually means a fairly big ceremony, and a big reception to follow.

The church ceremony isn't always possible or desirable, however. Couples may be new to an area and may not yet be associated with a church or synagogue. Fees get steep for non-members, so a local house of worship unfamiliar to the couple might not be worth the expense. The couple may be from different faiths and may not have time to scout for a non-denominational church (most go for justice of the peace weddings). Or they may simply want to have their ceremony in a different setting, the choice of which is limited only by the imagination.

Some brides and grooms charter yachts for the ceremony and reception. They set up huge tents in national parks. They rent mansions or country clubs. They have small ceremonies and receptions at home, or at restaurants, farms, beaches or ski resorts. For some, a chapel wedding ceremony does the trick and for others taking their vows in a hot air balloon beats the band.

The possibilities for ceremony sites are limitless. However, a general rule is that having the ceremony at the same site as the reception saves money, unless you choose an outdoor wedding, always a costly option. It's also a lot more convenient and takes less time to have your ceremony at a luxury hotel or country club with a reception to immediately follow.

Keep the arrangements as simple and conventional as possible; different costs more in most cases. And don't forget time of year, day, time, and type of reception rest in part on how you handle your ceremony. Think of the ceremony and reception plans as a single unit, and see how one set of options influences another from a cost standpoint.

The Reception

Sharing your special moment at the ceremony with family and friends, and having a big party afterward repeats an age-old ritual.

The reception carries with it a heavy weight of traditions. First dances, the cake-cutting, garter and bouquet tossing, the leave-taking as the couple dashes away for their romantic honeymoon are the things a great wedding is made of, at least for most couples. Taking part in the traditions of weddings is what makes them so special—the couple joins a long continuum of those who went before and will come afterward.

The reception of choice still remains one held in the evening with a great meal, music, a big wedding cake, and lots of dancing and fun—all recorded in photographs and on video. Some brides and grooms do it differently and save thousands of dollars, but according to industry experts the axiom "if you're gonna do it once, do it right" stands as firmly rooted in the minds of contemporary couples as it has for hundreds of years. And why not. A wedding day is special; it should be a time for making merry.

Receptions account for by far, the most costly of wedding items, consuming between 30 to 40 percent of the total budget, and the number of things which influence price can make your head spin. Here are just some of them: type of reception and location; time of year and day it's held; whether it's held on a weekend or weeknight; the music, flowers, food and drinks; the length and number of guests; and various services from bartenders to busboys.

Food and drinks account for the largest portion of the reception expenses. Prices increase as the day goes on, from breakfast starting at the least costly to evenings at the head of the list. A breakfast, brunch or lunch reception, particularly if it's kept small (fifty to seventy-five guests), can be self-catered or partially catered. The larger dinners begin to get so labor-intensive that it's best to pay professionals, and prices go up across the board when you do.

A sit-down dinner reception held on a weeknight could cost as much as 50 percent less than one with the same menu and number of guests held on a Saturday night. A shorter cocktail reception starting at nine o'clock will cost far less than a dinner reception which starts at six and won't end until eleven. Shortening the duration of the reception can mean significant savings.

If you keep an open mind, you can find many ways to have a perfectly wonderful reception that won't cost you a bundle. Let's take a look at the types of receptions and locations to get a feel for them.

Types of Receptions and Locations

The Breakfast Reception
This is the least costly for obvious reasons. Bacon and eggs,

fruit, pastries, coffee and tea costs a fraction of what you'd pay for steak and an open bar for your guests. Preparation is easier and less time-consuming as well. A buffet style with an omelette chef is the most common.

Champagne or sparkling wine is sometimes served for the toast. Other than that, no alcohol is expected or needed. With a breakfast reception, you reap a substantial savings on two of the most expensive reception budget subcategories: food and alcohol.

But you also save on music (hardly anyone hires a band or DJ, though sometimes a pianist or harpist plays). Flowers aren't needed or if you want them, they needn't be as abundant. Many limousine service companies offer 10 percent discounts for morning weddings.

You might think an early ceremony with a mid-morning breakfast reception is bordering on going over the top with the cheapskate approach, but it really isn't. In fact, it offers the added bonus of leaving you free to fly off to your honeymoon destination in the afternoon, leaving your wedding night free. Saving money and adding convenience and romance…not a bad payoff for flexibility.

In the 1990s, traditions are being reshaped to fit changing lifestyles. Having a breakfast reception can allow you to pay for many of the other traditional things you want for your wedding or for a nicer honeymoon.

SIZE: generally small (fifty to seventy-five guests)
STYLE: informal, semiformal

Held mostly in restaurants, hotels, banquet or church halls, fraternal organizations, sometimes at home.

Brunch or Lunch Reception
These are a little more expensive because in most cases alcohol is served and the menus get a little more complicated, involving expensive items such as meats. The good news about the alcohol? You can get away with alcoholic punch instead of mixed drinks, which is much cheaper.

And those expensive meats? You're talking roast beef, ham, and turkey breast—that kind of fare—at a carving station...no gourmet hors d'oeuvres or individual dinners. Site rates are less than for evenings.

Variations on the brunch or lunch receptions are afternoon teas, punch and cake receptions, pig roasts, lobster bakes, fish fries, picnics, and many others.

SIZE: fifty guests and up
STYLE: informal, semiformal

Held mostly in restaurants, hotels, banquet or church halls, fraternal organizations, country clubs, mansions, sometimes on yachts, outdoors, and at home.

Cocktail-Only Reception

The cocktail-only reception is a creature of the 1990s, gaining in acceptance as the decade progresses. Many couples would just like a big party to celebrate their marriage, not a formal reception with all the trimmings. With the right crowd, the cocktail reception can be a great success. The reception is kept short, around two or three hours, and the cake-cutting ceremony is the culminating event.

This approach eliminates the full meal in favor of tasty tidbits. No flowers are needed to adorn dozens of dining and serving tables. A full dance band hired for half the time (check about minimums), or DJ costs 25 to 40 percent less. String quartets, harpists, and other musicians who often don't have minimums cost around $250 to $300 for a two- to three-hour engagement, as opposed to wedding bands which start at around $1,500 for four-hour gigs. Serve coffee, tea, and soft drinks during the last hour, which saves on alcohol fees and promotes safe driving.

Unfortunately, a downside exists with the cocktail-only reception. You'll find that some people who you've always thought were civil and well-mannered will drink a huge amount of alcohol and hog the hors d'oeuvres. There is a weird thing about guests. They expect a meal and if they don't get one they transform into finger-food gluttons. Of course not everyone behaves this way, but these are a few land mines you might encounter with the cocktail-only reception.

SIZE: ten guests and up
STYLE: formal to informal; late afternoons, evenings

Held in hotels, banquet halls, fraternal organizations, church halls, mansions, country clubs, yacht clubs, yachts, sometimes outdoors, and at home.

Evening Receptions

These are the most common and most expensive receptions, involving the most of everything from goods to services. In the 1990s, serving stations and buffet presentations are far more accepted today than in the past. These eliminate paying for waiter and waitress services. Foods are also simpler and less expensive.

If you're going to go for this kind of reception, your best bet for savings is to choose an off-season month, have your reception on a weeknight or on Friday night, hire a DJ instead of a band, and serve the least expensive foods. Shop around very carefully for the most attractive deal you can find. When you choose the formal evening reception, you're doing what more than 95 percent of all couples do. When you go with the herd, you pay more.

SIZE: twenty and up
STYLE: formal to informal

Held in hotels, banquet halls, fraternal organizations, church halls, mansions, country clubs, yacht clubs, yachts, sometimes outdoors, and at home.

Cost-Saving Tips

Go with a simple, good dinner. Avoid complicated dishes, expensive ingredients, and more difficult preparations.

If you must include delicacies like wild mushrooms or seafood, serve them as hors d'oeuvres, not the main course. This reduces costs by lowering use of expensive ingredients.

Serve an alcoholic punch at the reception instead of having an open bar.

Serve sparkling wine instead of champagne for the toast.

Have a tea reception with pastries and cakes, teas and coffees. No meal or alcohol bills.

Make your own wedding cake or include sheet cake in design to lower costs.

Seafood and beef are the most expensive meats; don't serve them. Try less costly chicken and turkey, pastas, and salads.

Go with a buffet or serving stations instead of table service. This saves on service charges for waiters and waitresses.

Hire a DJ instead of a band.

Use a single or a handful of flowers with baby's breath for table centerpieces. Or buy the flowers and arrange them yourself. Use silk flowers instead of live ones, if you can get them at a reasonable price.

Use potted flowers for serving table decorations or eliminate flowers altogether.

Use decorative candles instead of flowers for centerpieces.

Make your own food and buy your own liquor, when feasible. For at-home weddings, or sites such as church halls. Small guest list.

Establishments with in-house catering often don't charge a site fee if you use the catering services. But compare costs for in-house versus bringing in an off-premises caterer.

CHAPTER
14

Flowers: Finding Your Way Through the Financial Weeds

How many times have you seen that hackneyed old scene in B movies where a long separated couple runs across a field of flowers to embrace? Usually, the film directors capture the romantic moment in slow motion...the camera zooms in for a close-up of the passionate kiss, then fades.

The field of flowers symbolizes the couple's love, serving as a visual backdrop to something intangible but as beautiful as a flower. At a wedding, the flowers also symbolize the couple's love and serve as a visual backdrop to help create a special mood for everyone at the celebration.

Few events require as much in the way of flowers as a traditional wedding. Here's what you'll need:

- Floral arrangements to decorate the ceremony site
- Bouquets for the bride and her attendants
- Possibly a throwaway bouquet
- Boutonnieres for the groom, male attendants, and fathers of the bride and groom
- Corsages for mothers of the bride and groom
- Centerpieces for the dining and serving tables at the reception

- Flowers for others such as grandparents, flower girls, pages, and flowers to decorate guest book location, restrooms, bandstand, and so on

The whole floral package for most weddings usually runs from $700 to $1,000 on average, throughout the nation. But the variability of the flower market makes it very difficult to peg prices. The supply and demand factor which influences all businesses enters heavily into the picture. To get the best deal, you'll need to turn the whims of the market in your favor.

Although prices do vary, the following will provide a rough guideline on what you'll spend at the low end of the market with relatively inexpensive flowers:

- Bride's bouquet: $80 and up
- Table centerpiece: $30 and up
- Flower baskets for church: $50 and up
- Boutonnieres and corsages: $8 and up

Seasonal Influences on Price

Naturally, when flowers are plentiful in your region during a given season the price will be lower than when the supply dwindles. When working with your florist, find out which flowers will be in season on your wedding day and which flowers are grown locally, preferably in your state. Use these flowers in your floral arrangements.

If you plan to include exotic flowers such as orchids, stephanotis, lilies and others, ask your florist which type will be least expensive at the time of your wedding. Exotic flowers must be shipped to your location, which adds to the expense. If the flowers you choose aren't readily available, the price will be high.

Avoiding the More Expensive Holiday Months

You'll find inflated flower prices because of high demand during any major holiday month. Growers raise their prices to florists and florists pass the hikes along, often with additional hefty markups to take advantage of a hot selling period. If you love roses and want them for your wedding, don't get married in February when every guy in the country is buying roses for his true love on St. Valentine's Day. You'll pay as much as 300 percent more for your roses than you would during a nonholiday month.

Most couples don't think about such seemingly unconnected details as holidays and flower prices, and how these will impact on the costs for the wedding. When planning your date, be aware of the supply and demand factor across the board, and flowers are no exception. St. Valentine's Day in February, Easter in March or April, Mother's Day in May, Father's Day in June, and the Christmas holiday season are months where you can expect inflated flower prices. Prices tend to drop about 10 percent during the summer months when demand is lower.

The Much Cheaper Nursery

While the florist offering wonderful arrangements of cut flowers remains the norm for most weddings, an increasing number of couples are buying less expensive live potted plants at nurseries for some of their floral needs. Potted plants, by the way, don't come in those clunky clay pots with tacky red foil wrapped around them. They are tastefully designed plantings with ivy, ferns, Spanish moss, and other adornments.

Consider a pretty basket of potted seasonal flowering plants for reception centerpieces instead of the grand pedestal arrangement of cut roses or exotic flowers. For a winter wedding, try a basket with pink and white azalea decorated with needlepoint ivy, or in spring, geraniums of the same color. In fall, yellow daisy baskets capture the feel of the season. Baskets start on average at around $30. Depending on where you live, you can probably do even better.

Spend $30 on a basket and you'll receive a simple yet elegant centerpiece which doesn't look cheap. If you spend $30 on a centerpiece of cut flowers, you won't get more than a handful with lots of baby's breath to fill it out; it'll look skimpy. Also, your potted flowers won't die during the festivities and you can give them to attendants as gifts or take them home with you.

Topiaries are another cost-saving option for your centerpieces. A topiary is a planting trimmed or grown into a special shape. Your nursery can supply topiaries of needlepoint ivy in the shape of a heart or a circle; you can put a candle in the center to create a simple but beautiful look. A topiary starts as low as $15.

Let's take a quick look at numbers. If you've got ten tables for guests and your cut flower centerpieces cost $50 each, not an ungodly sum, you've just rung up a $500 bill for that component alone. If you go with topiaries priced at $15 each you'll pay $150, saving you a hefty $350. Is it worth several hundred dollars to you to have cut flowers when you can go with an alternative which won't look cheap and yet costs 70 percent less?

Here's another example: Go with carnations for boutonnieres and corsages. It's an inexpensive flower and will lower costs. A florist charging $15 for a carnation corsage will charge around $27 for one made from a large orchid, just to give you an idea of the price spread. When you select flowers wisely and with a firm grasp of costs instead of relying solely on your emotions, you can save money and still have beautiful flowers at the wedding

When and How to Get Started

It's time to find a florist as soon as the bride selects her gown and knows her wedding colors for bridesmaids gowns, and the couple selects the reception site and knows the size of the wedding party. There's not much point in starting before that since the colors chosen for the wedding will directly influence what types of flowers you'll choose. The reception site's size and setting, the wedding style and number of guests will also come into play.

At the minimum, start looking for your florist at least four months ahead of the wedding date. If you're planning your wedding for a peak month, contact a florist eight months to a year in advance.

The next step is to familiarize yourself with the floral arrangements you see in bridal magazines. You'll find very elegant and complicated designs which would break anyone on a low budget, but if you find something you like cut the page out and show it to your florist. Discuss how the design could be made simpler and with less expensive flowers.

Drop by your local florists and check out their catalogs. These are much like the huge books of wedding stationery found at printers, bridal shops, and other stores. You'll find virtually any kind of floral arrangement with every conceivable theme and variation. Again, show the florist what you like and ask for a price based on less expensive flower substitutions.

When you visit your florist for an initial consultation, bring a color swatch of your bridesmaids gowns. The flowers you choose will have to work well with the wedding colors, and having a swatch for the florist will help you make the right selection.

What to Expect

Most florists include the labor of arranging the flowers, delivery, and setup in the price. They also often include accessories as part of their services such as flower containers and stands, pew markers, candles, and aisle runners. Ask about these items when you make your preliminary calls. Also, try to select a florist close to your ceremony and reception site; travel time can cost $40 an hour, plus mileage.

Make sure to get everything in writing before you hand over a check.

Other Cost-Saving Tips

The cost of flowers adds up. You don't just need one bouquet, boutonniere, corsage, or centerpiece, you need flowers for the entire wedding party. Big weddings have big wedding parties and big bills for flowers. If you have a small wedding, you'll escape the costly multiplicity factor

Save 50 percent off flowers for the wedding ceremony by getting together with another bride being married at the site on the same day. Ask if other weddings are scheduled at the ceremony site on your wedding day and get in touch with the other couple to see if they'd like to split ceremony flower costs. You'll need to work out budgets, colors, timing, etc.

It's customary to donate flowers used at a ceremony held in a house of worship, but couples sometimes take them to the reception site. Getting double duty out of the arrangments will save money, particularly if you work with your florist on altar decorations which can easily work as serving table pieces or in other ways.

Be wary of silk flowers. Low quality silks will be cheaper than cut flowers, and they'll look it. High quality silks which look real cost as much or more than cut flowers. Some brides like silk because the flowers last forever.

Have your ceremony and reception in an outdoor garden at a restaurant, country club, or country mansion. You can greatly reduce the quantity of flowers needed to create the special mood.

Don't buy floral centerpieces. Use decorative candles instead.

Instead of buying a cheap throwaway bouquet, ask the florist to design a detachable portion of the bridal bouquet which can be thrown away, allowing you to save the remainder as a keepsake.

Take advantage of giveaways and price discounts offered in bridal guide ads.

Carry a prayer book decorated with flowers instead of a

bouquet. Use single flower presentations for maid of honor and bridesmaids.

Wear a simple flower wreath instead of paying for a headpiece.

At some small, informal weddings the groomsmen wear white handkerchiefs in breast pockets instead of boutonnieres.

Package deals aren't always the least expensive because they limit your options. Sometimes it's best to work one-on-one with your florist to tailor the flowers to your budget rather than select a cheap package. You can get more for your money with a creative florist willing to help.

Some couples let bridesmaids bouquets do double duty as decorations for the head table, eliminating the costs for some centerpieces.

CHAPTER
15

The Music

Music touches people's hearts and inspires memories every time a favorite song plays on the radio or stereo. Those corny TV ads for nostalgia records of hits during the 1950s through the 1980s appeal to memory by tugging on sentimental feelings. They allow listeners to sample an audio blast from the past, which triggers a flood of images and thoughts meaningful only to them.

Taken in the context of marriage, the same links between music and memory apply. Most couples have a favorite song, usually the one they danced to or enjoyed when they first met. Hearing it inspires memories of falling in love and all the joy of that special time.

The music at the ceremony and, more important, at the reception will live on long after the wedding day in your memories and in the memories of your guests. If you have a video done with an audio track of the wedding, it will also live on in a very tangible sense (many videos don't use actual audio throughout; instead, there is usually a taped music soundtrack). The music will set the tone of the day and get the party rolling. It's one of the most important considerations during the wedding planning process.

The Ceremony

Music at the ceremony ranges from the traditional organ to violins and harps at sites not affiliated with a religion. The church or synagogue probably has a specified set of rules about music for the ceremony that the couple must follow. The expense for these services is usually very low because the church or temple's musicians come as part of the package.

At ceremonies held outside a religious venue, the couple has no limitations. In cases where funds are tight, the music at the ceremony can be a tape recording of classical music, New Age music, nature sounds, or whatever appeals to the couple. Select appropriate music for background before the ceremony, the processional, and recessional.

As a rule of thumb, the cheapskate approach would avoid hiring string quartets or other live players for the ceremony. It's not the best place to spend a lot of money on music. Although music is important to the ceremony, going the simple way to lower overall costs won't hurt the quality of the moment. Most guests don't pay much attention to the music at ceremonies. They're too excited about seeing you take your vows.

The Reception

Bands

Bands are still very popular, particularly at upscale celebrations. They have the advantage of adding the dynamics of live performances and visual appeal to the reception, and they can get the crowd out on the dance floor and keep them there. A good band leader can read the audience and create excitement or a more subdued feel at various points throughout the reception.

But bands cost a considerable amount of money. The average price for a band runs between $1,500 and $3,500. You'll also pay travel expenses such as a mileage fee and overtime costs if the reception goes longer than planned. When selecting a band, try to find one that won't have to travel for hours to get to your reception site. This will save money.

If you're booking a reception site at a hotel, country club, or restaurant, ask the provider to recommend bands in the area. Contact booking agencies or bands from the phone book covering the area immediately around the site.

The vocalist is the most important part of the band. He or she will have limitations in the styles of music that can be played. A great jazz vocalist may well have trouble doing a country and western song. When selecting a band, make sure the vocalist can sing in the style you want and make sure the band plays together all the time. Some don't. Rather, the band is cobbled together at the last minute by the booking agency.

The music on the play list should be eclectic, covering a broad range of tunes to appeal to all ages. Ethnic tunes that the couple and their families would appreciate can also be included. Not everyone will like each tune because of generational differences in musical tastes. The idea is to choose music that will please the majority of guests.

Some couples like to hire bands specializing in a specific style such as jazz, country, or rock. But most want the all-around versatility of a wedding band, which can play a wide variety of popular top forty, golden oldies, wedding dance songs, and ethnic tunes.

Whether you hire a DJ or a band, provide a list of songs you definitely want played. If you don't want certain songs or tunes played, like the Electric Slide (a popular dance piece), make sure you let the band or DJ know. Some entertainers provide play lists from which the couple can make selections; others don't.

Always give the band or DJ some leeway to improvise. Locking them into a specified list of tunes to be played in a specific sequence robs them of the ability to work the crowd, something you're relying on and paying for.

DJs

DJs offer advantages of their own. They cost a fraction of what a six-piece band charges for obvious reasons: fewer people, less overhead. The average cost for a good DJ is around $500, though some charge a little more. You'll find that virtually anyone can hang out a shingle saying they're a professional DJ, and some charge a lot less than the average of $500. Watch out if that's the case. As with every other budget category, don't let price be the sole determining factor on whom you hire.

Advantages: the DJ doesn't take breaks, so you'll have non-stop music. Since you're hearing the original artists performing their tunes, the songs will sound the same way you're used to hearing them. Many couples don't like hearing a band's interpretation of songs by their favorite artists because the tune often loses something in the translation.

When selecting a DJ, make sure his or her stage personality suits your tastes. The DJ acts as the master of ceremonies, just like a band leader. But since the DJ is all alone, or with an assistant, he or she will need to be dynamic and fun.

Make sure the DJ's equipment is top-flight. For example, does the compact disc player have a suspension system to avoid skips when the dance floor is full?

Band and DJ Combo

Hiring a combination of a band and DJ is becoming more popular these days. The combo gives the reception the best of both worlds—the dynamics of live performers and songs by original artists. The rates for a combo can be reasonable when booked through agencies specializing in such packages. You can hire a three-piece band and a DJ for about what you'd pay a reasonably priced band. Prices start at around $1,500, depending on location.

The One-Man Band

The image you might have of a one-man band probably

springs from cartoons of a funny looking guy with cymbals between his knees, a foot-operated bass drum, an accordian around his neck, and various wind instruments suspended off hangers around his head. Today's one-man bands aren't like that at all.

In fact, with today's technology, you can hire a one-man band and still get great music. The one-man band will have a synthesizer which can lay down percussion, horns, and other background arrangements. The performer superimposes his "live" playing and vocals over the "canned" arrangements. He or she can also perform solo numbers. In some cases, he or she will also act as a DJ, piping compact disc recordings through the sound system.

The one-man band can be somewhat limiting, and if he or she isn't a real pro, the one-man band can be downright hilarious...if it's not *your* wedding reception that's ruined. The right one-man band is a good, inexpensive way to go if you want the dynamics of a live performer but don't want to spend a couple thousand dollars. Travel expenses are also less with a one-man band.

Just be extra careful to thoroughly audition him or her before deciding to go this route.

Harps, Trumpets, and Other Variations

At receptions without dancing, such as a plush dinner or an outdoor wedding in the garden of a mansion, some couples like the touch of class that classical musicians can add. Acoustic, natural music combined with an elegant setting creates a special mood unique from the party type associated with bands and DJs. It's also less expensive than bands, about equal to the cost of a DJ.

The Booking Agent

You can find bands or DJs listed in the phone book, in ads from newspaper wedding sections, and regional bridal guides. Word of mouth is a sound (pun intended) way to go about finding a band or DJ.

Many individual bands or DJs work through a booking agency. The agency handles them, provides scheduling, and other services such as showcases. When dealing with a booking agency, make sure it's a licensed operation if your state regulates entertainment companies. Cover all the fine points of the contract.

Just because you heard and liked a band and hired it at a showcase doesn't mean that particular one will show up on your wedding day unless you specify it in the contract. Many a couple has loved a band at a showcase only to find a band they had never heard or seen show up at the reception.

The contract should include items such as the name of band or DJ hired (in addition to the agency if appropriate, and names of band members); time, place, and duration of the gig; time and number of breaks as well as any applicable overtime charges; cancellation policy, and expected attire of performers.

Most booking agencies hold a showcase night once or twice a month. The bands and DJs play for about twenty minutes. Couples get to see them perform outside the context of a specific wedding, which is an advantage. You can't always tell how good a band or DJ is in a "hot" audition, one where the crowd impacts on the performance. Every crowd is different, and so are performances.

Yet, some couples want to see bands or DJs in action. There are cases where couples show up at a stranger's wedding to hear the band or DJ in a "hot" audition. This is not a good idea for the reasons mentioned already. (But also how would you like it if strangers showed up at your reception? There are even cases where the strangers wore jeans with holes in the knees and helped themselves to the open bar!)

Sometimes the band, DJ, or booking agency will offer you an audio tape or a video in lieu of a showcase or a "hot" audition. These methods are okay. However, a live audition at a showcase or, failing that, at a nightclub (never someone else's wedding) where the performer has a gig is best.

Other Musical Options

Even though this book is about the "cheapskate" approach to weddings and honeymoons, there comes a point where it's dangerous to be too cheap. The following suggestions may work for some folks, but they should be used only with the utmost caution. Music is too important to risk embarrassment. Most any couple can afford $500 for a DJ or a one-man band, so go with that if you can't afford a large wedding band.

Cost-Saving Tips

Hire college or high school students to play at the reception. Music majors or good part-time musicians with talent want experience and they're generally pretty hungry for cash. You can hire them for a fraction of what you'd pay a professional band.

You may decide to hedge your bets and hire a DJ, but let student musicians fill in for some of the reception. A good student pianist or string quartet, for example, can play during the dinner hour. The DJ takes over after that.

Ask friends who are musicians to play at the reception. Their providing music could be your wedding gift. The downside is they may join in the celebration (who could blame them?) and not play as much as you bargained for.

Tape your own music and have a friend switch tapes as needed. This might work out for a small wedding, but you'll be missing the dynamics of a good performer without a DJ or band which is so important to get the party rolling at larger receptions. The reception could fall flat. It may even be boring.

If you don't have dancing at the reception, hire a harpist or string quartet for an hour or two, and end with the cake-cutting. This is a viable plan, but it's much more fun to have dancing. Besides, hiring a live player even for an hour or two will still cost you around $250 or so.

Don't have music. If you're only having a small gathering in a restaurant, you may get away without music, though even then it'll hurt the feel of the reception. For most couples, their wedding reception will be a much more elaborate celebration, making music a necessity.

16

Photographs for Posterity

As you turn the pages of your wedding album years after your celebration, memories of that special day will come flooding back: the joy and happiness, the anticipation and excitement. That's the magic of good wedding photography; the images capture the cherished moments so you can relive them again and again.

Photography is a subjective business and as much an art as a science. The lighting, composition, contrast in the photos, camera angle, types of cameras and film, and most important, the skill of the photographer all come together to form the basic ingredients of what determines whether the photographs will look good or bad. Standards vary widely among photographers, as do prices.

The average couple spending a total of $10,000 on their wedding spends approximately $1,000 to $1,500 for still photography. The typical package includes four or five hours of coverage, film developing, proofs, eighty to one hundred and fifty prints of various sizes, and a leather wedding album. This price range will provide you with mid-market quality photographers in most locations throughout the country.

On the East and West Coasts in suburban and urban areas, mid-market prices sometimes increase to $2,000 to $2,500. In

Chicago, $2,000 to $2,500 will buy top market quality, and in the South top market photographers can be had for $1,000. In every market, you'll find prices spread across the board with rates starting as low as $200.

What do you get for $200? Not much. Say one hour of coverage for the ceremony, portrait shots of the bride and groom, attendants, and family members. Sometimes the fee includes developing film at a one-hour photo lab and an album containing about thirty photographs. For some couples, wedding photographs aren't that important and a few reasonably well-shot images of the moment are all that's required.

Low-budget photographers with an unscrupulous nature often advertise cheap packages as a form of bait to lure couples into a contract. Be very wary of hidden charges listed in the fine print, and if you don't find fine details in the contract, spell out your expectations, together with agreed upon fees, and add them as an addendum to the document. You may be charged extra money for cropping, enlargements, travel time, overtime, and other items which would be included in more expensive packages.

If you can't afford the $1,000 to $1,500 for complete wedding photography service, there is one good way out. It takes some work on your part, but you save lots of loot. Pay a photographer just for his or her time—typically $300 or $400 for two to three hours. He or she will give you the film and bow out of the process, leaving you to handle film development, ordering reprints, and compiling the album for you and your friends. These folks aren't as common as the types who want to handle the whole thing from soup to nuts, but they're around in every market.

It's worth noting that photographers who work on a pay-for-time basis aren't necessarily inferior to their counterparts offering comprehensive service. They're less expensive because they're not providing the full range of services, just the most important one: taking good pictures of your wedding.

Another cost-saving method is to contact professional color labs in your area to see if they know any up-and-coming photographers who are new to the wedding market and looking for recognition. It's worth a few calls to try to find such an individual because if he or she is talented, you'll get top-flight service for a fraction of what an established wedding photographer would charge.

How to Find and Choose a Wedding Photographer

As always, word of mouth is the best way to find a trustworthy wedding professional in your area. If none of your friends have gotten married recently and can't give you a referral, call wedding professionals in your area such as consultants, caterers, florists, musicians, and others for recommendations. If all else fails, let your fingers go walking through the phone book.

Next, look at ads in wedding sections of major newspapers and in regional bridal guides. Some large studios also advertise in major bridal magazines. Look for ads which address price in some way, such as offering freebies, flexible prices, photography packages for every budget, that kind of thing. Unless you want up-market prices, avoid the type of ad which looks elegant, has very little copy, and says absolutely nothing about price.

When you start calling, keep in mind that your objective is to get an idea of where the photographer's prices stand relative to the overall prevailing rates in your market area. You'll need to make a number of calls to survey the market. Tell the photographers you're on a very low budget and get them to spell out their most basic package and everything it includes. You may find some photographers won't be specific and instead will ask you to come in to see their work. Move on to someone else at this stage.

After you feel you have a fairly good take on prices in your area for the most basic package, make a couple of appointments to see photographers whom you liked dealing with over the phone, and who offered fair prices. Make sure that when you look at the studio's work, you get the name of the photographer who took the photographs and that he or she is the one who will be shooting your wedding. As with bands, sometimes you don't get the person whose work you liked; a different, unknown individual shows up, and that's unpleasant and annoying.

As you speak with the photographer, it's vital that you feel comfortable with his or her personality. The photographer will spend a lot of time with you and your family and closest friends throughout the wedding day. The comfort factor is almost as important as the monetary considerations.

If you like the photographer and his or her pictures, go ahead and take a copy of their contract home. Give the matter some thought before signing. You should start looking for a photographer as far in advance as possible to ensure the one you like will be available on your date.

After the wedding, you should receive your proofs in roughly two to three weeks. The delivery of photo albums varies. Two months isn't uncommon. Most major studios keep the negatives. Ask about their policies as well as any reprint charges in case you decide you want more photos later.

On Film: 35 mm or "Medium Format"

Wedding photographers traditionally use what's known as medium format film. The negatives are two inches square, to allow for better enlargements and provide better quality reproduction than 35 mm films. Medium format photographers will be more expensive.

Advances in 35 mm film in the last ten to fifteen years have begun to erase the quality difference between that and medium format film. A good comparison might be engraving versus thermography for invitations. Due to advances in technology, less costly thermography is just about as good as engraving. The same goes for 35 mm film—it's just about as good as medium format and it takes an expert to tell the difference in most cases.

The Photojournalist Approach

Although most couples hire professional wedding photographers, some adventurous brides and grooms of the 1990s are trying something new: the photojournalist approach. Perhaps it might be right for you, too, if you prefer action shots instead of posed images typical of traditional albums. The resulting album still tells the story of the wedding, but often in more eye-catching, provocative ways.

This approach can reduce what would have been a $1,000 wedding fee paid to a wedding photography specialist to roughly $100 to $150. How? Because you've placed a lower value on having a traditional type of wedding album, you can take advantage of buying photography services outside the wedding market. Go straight to your local weekly newspaper and ask for the names of any freelance photographers in the area or if their staff photographer takes on outside jobs.

Since you don't expect or want slick and flashy traditional wedding photography, the skills of a good photojournalist are quite enough to ensure a nice spread of candids covering the entire celebration. Black and white photographs shot with 35 mm film are very popular with this approach.

The photojournalist can also take portraits and traditional photographs like the kiss, toast, or first dance. Outline the shots you want with the photographer ahead of time—just as you would with a wedding specialist.

Other Tips and Options

If you're compiling your own album, ask for one as a wedding gift.

A photographer who knows your wedding ceremony and reception site is helpful. He or she will know about lighting and other variables associated with the site.

Your photographer should bring an assistant to help with things such as setting up backdrops if they're needed or with additional lighting.

Have a friend who's an amateur photographer take pictures as his or her wedding gift to you.

Choose a photographer close to the ceremony and reception site to save travel time or mileage charges.

Limit the size of album, size of prints, number of shoot locations, and shy away from extra charges for cropping, enlargements, and "enchancements."

Names and Numbers

Most states or regions have their own photography associations, and there are national associations as well. Most will provide you with a referral to a member operating in your area.

For a referral to a photographer in your area specializing in weddings, call Wedding and Portrait Photographers International at (310) 451-0090.

CHAPTER
17

Video and Your Wedding

The last ten years have ushered in a new twist on weddings—the video. It's not likely that videos will ever replace stills, but the video has become as entrenched in wedding traditions as still photography. Some might argue videos already stand shoulder to shoulder with the wedding album in importance as an increasing number of brides and grooms hire video crews in addition to photographers. And maybe the prognosticators are right.

By the late 1980s, advances in video technology began to make it feasible to videotape weddings at a price the average couple could afford. Video cameras have gotten much smaller and easier to handle. Video quality has improved as the industry matures, and the equipment has become affordable to a larger number of would-be videographers. All these factors have steadily lowered the price for the video.

As a bride or groom of the 1990s, chances are you're going to want a wedding video, and you're probably wondering how much it will cost. Figure around $1,000, though you can downscale or eliminate the video to save money. If you're on a very tight budget, the video is one place where you can cut without losing all that much. The wedding album has been sufficient for ages, and it still is. But fewer and fewer couples see it that way.

Costs for wedding videos vary considerably by region. The average package for a sixty- to ninety-minute edited video with five hours of taping runs anywhere from $1,200 to $2,500 on the East and West Coasts, and from $750 to $1,000 in the Midwest and the South. Prices include a number of add-ons as well as setup and takedown charges.

If you live in rural areas of the country miles from suburbs and urban centers, you may not be able to find a videographer, and if you do, he or she will likely charge a fairly hefty fee due to a lack of competition in the area. Eventually, videographers will spread out across the country as the industry continues to grow, but for now they're most common near large populations capable of supporting the business.

You've probably heard of or seen some pretty awful wedding videos. The nightmares include unflattering close-ups, jerky camera motions, bad lighting, garbled audio, weird color distortions, sloppy editing, and just plain boring mumbo jumbo which doesn't fit together in any way. Even the couple yawns and presses the fast forward button. "Oh, that's a boring part, but wait, it gets better!" How many times have you squirmed after hearing that at a newly married friend or relative's video viewing?

Unfortunately, since the industry is still relatively new, videographers are a varied lot. Standards of quality, type of tape, the approach, the fee all vary. It helps to have some tips from an expert to guide you through the video for your wedding before picking up the phone to call your local videographer.

GETTING THE RIGHT WEDDING VIDEO

Bob Mehaffey has been in the video business in one way or another since the mid-1970s. He and his wife, Jo Ann, operate Mehaffey Multimedia Productions in Mandeville, Louisiana, just outside New Orleans. Bob and Jo Ann are the leaders for the Wedding and Event Videography Special Interest Group of the Association of Professional Videographers, a national trade organization. He answered some common questions.

Q. What's the first step I should consider when dealing with the video for my wedding?

A. Think about what type of wedding video you want. They're not all the same. Some are straight ceremony only videos, others cover both the ceremony and reception, and still others incorporate montages, statements from friends, baby and teen pictures of the bride and groom, and honeymoon pictures, to name just a few of the extras.

So, your first step is to decide how complicated you want to get on the length, and what kind of budget you have to work with. Generally, if you're on a low budget, you'll have a short, simple video of the ceremony without lots of special effects and other extras.

Q. How much does a ceremony-only video cost?

A. If you go with a ceremony-only video, including some well-wishes from close friends and a statement from the bride and groom, in our area the cost would be about $300 to $450. The average price in our area for more complex videos ranges from $750 to $850, and sometimes goes much higher. You'll find similar price differences among the various packages available elsewhere in the country, too.

The rule of thumb in saving costs is to keep the video as simple as possible. You can still have a very nice video which captures the magic of the wedding even without the extras. It all depends on the expertise and creative ability of your videographer.

Q. Are there any other ways to save money?

A. As I've said, prices vary considerably. If you look around, you'll find the lowest prices in your area. Shopping for the best price can save money. But don't shop price alone because the lowest price might not result in a good wedding video.

There are part-time videographers in most major areas, though they're hard to find. They'll charge about 50 percent less than a full-time professional. Sometimes they're good, experienced videographers just looking to pay off a camera or to break into the business full-time, and they're well worth the price. Others aren't so good.

You might try calling local ad agencies and colleges which offer videography courses to find local part-time videographers. Again, just be sure you're comfortable with the risk; if the person messes up, you don't have another take.

Q. How do I find a videographer for my wedding?

A. You can find wedding videographers in regional bridal guides, wedding ad sections of major newspapers, at bridal shows, and in the phone book. Referrals from friends or wedding professionals are best. Try to hire a videographer who's close to the ceremony and reception site to avoid travel charges.

Q. Okay, so I've got a few names. I'm ready to call, but what do I ask and how do I know if he or she is any good?

A. Call and say you're shopping around for a videographer, and ask about their least expensive package. Get price quotes from a couple of others in the area for similar packages and compare prices. When you've found a company you think you may feel comfortable with, which can deliver the video you want at a price you've confirmed is fair, call back and ask some more questions.

For example, ask if the company will send two videographers. More than one camera is important, especially at a large event. Also, ask if the company uses super VHS (Video Home System tape format). Some use standard VHS, which isn't as good.

Ask about the audio. Does the price include musical soundtracks or just an ambient approach which picks up the sounds in the room? Does the price include attending the rehearsal? It's vital for the videographer to work out the technical details before the wedding day, so he or she can address any problems which might interfere with making the best video possible.

Finally, the videographer should belong to a professional association and have years of experience in the video business. He or she should have attended seminars or have some other training in the wedding video business.

If you like what you've heard, go check out the company's videos. Just remember, they're showing you their best stuff; ask to see more than one or two tapes.

Q. What makes a good video? What should I look for when I see sample videos?

A. Set your standards according to what you're used to seeing on TV. You'll see a solid shot with no camera jerks. People move smoothly in and out of frame. The lighting should be balanced and adequate, and the audio should not be distracting or garbled.

Also, the video should tell a story of the wedding, capture all the feelings that transpire that day and present it all in a cohesive manner. If the sample video falls short in what you see, you can bet your video will probably have the same problems.

Q. How long does it take to set up a video shoot for a wedding?

A. It takes us about two hours to set up in most cases.

Q. Should I book far in advance?

A. Definitely. The best videographers are usually booked about a year in advance. Look for your videographer as early on in the process as possible.

Q. Why is it important for the videographer to attend the rehearsal?

A. Usually, the rehearsal is part of the package. The videographer has to address concerns about lighting, camera positions, and other factors. For instance, it sometimes comes up at the rehearsal that the minister won't allow wireless microphones, which might interfere with the church's own system, or no cameras are allowed near the altar, things like that.

You don't want any surprises on the wedding day, so that's why your videographer should attend the rehearsal. He or she's got to have a good understanding of what needs to be done beforehand to ensure conditions are as good as possible for shooting a video.

Q. Is editing included in the price?

A. Usually. But make sure to ask. If the company charges an hourly rate for editing on top of what sounded like a great price on a basic package, you could end up spending a lot of money you hadn't counted on. It takes about twelve to twenty-five hours on average to edit a relatively problem-free sixty-minute video. It can take sixty hours if lots of problems came up, though that's unusual.

Q. Is making a good wedding video hard?

A. Yes, it can be challenging. The videographer has marginal control over lighting, audio, and other elements you'd normally consider as rudimentary to making good videos. You have only one opportunity to capture the event, usually under trying conditions. But even with the occasional difficulties, making wedding videos is a lot of fun.

CHAPTER
18

Cheapskate Weddings

The Chapel Wedding

The minister looks and sounds like a used car salesman. The bride's wearing too much makeup, and the groom's sharkskin suit doesn't fit. Canned organ music groans in the background as the couple take their vows.

After the ceremony, the couple retires to the honeymoon shack in the yard behind the chapel. A few other honeymoon bungalows nestle in the pines nearby.

Welcome to chapel country, pard. You ain't seen nothin' yet!

Those jokes about chapels are true, unfortunately. You don't have to look hard at this section of the wedding market to find some pretty hilarious brochures hyping some of the cheapest, most awful-looking weddings imaginable. Some of the material is even depressing...do people really go for this stuff?

You can find these places scattered across our great land from Florida to California. They cater to the eloping couple, and as a consequence they're located at major tourist spots and destinations known for honeymooners such as the Pocono Mountains, Las Vegas, and Lake Tahoe.

Competition for business among these providers is cutthroat because more than 90 percent of the weddings held each year are traditional, complete with religious ceremony followed by a sit-down dinner reception. That leaves less than 10 percent of the market for nontraditional weddings, such as those for couples who choose to elope. You can turn the competitive nature of the chapel business to your advantage. Shop around, and if possible, try to see the place in person.

You can get your whole wedding for around $200 at some of the low-budget chapels. The packages usually include the chapel, the minister, marriage license, honeymoon suite (usually with a heart-shaped tub), free champagne, a rose for the bride, a boutonniere for the groom, and even twenty-four prints of the glorious event.

But let the buyer beware. Some chapel operators will have all sorts of add-on services and fees. If you look around you'll notice that besides the site fee, many will charge you by the head for guests, force you to use their photographers or charge you a fee for not using them, and even charge you for plunking a tape of the Wedding March into a boom box. When you start shopping around, ask about all these charges.

Chapels often offer services for outdoor weddings. This is usually the case in highly scenic locations. The charges for this are sometimes lower than chapel site fees.

In fairness to the chapel entrepreneurs who do run nice operations, not every one of these businesses are a joke. Some are even quite refined and accordingly expensive at around $1,000 or more for a small wedding with a catered reception. For some couples, the chapel wedding, if it's tastefully done, is a great way to save money. You'll spend a fraction of the cost for a big wedding and you'll start your honeymoon right away with money in your pocket.

Chapel Tips

Find a chapel which charges a flat rate for the site, not one with a sliding price scale based on the total number of guests.

Find a chapel where you can take your own pictures. Photography add-ons are costly at a minimum of $100, and you have no idea of how good the photographer is.

Scrimp on flowers. Buy the basic three-rose bouquet or simple cascade for the bride.

Find a chapel which has a reception hall and allows self-catering. Bring your own food and liquor.

Try to see the place first and if this is impossible (it often is). Study the brochures. You may want to go with a chapel at a large resort to ensure quality, even if it costs more.

Price rooms at nice hotels and resorts near the chapel. The quality may be better for the same price than with what you get for the chapel wedding package which includes a "honeymoon suite."

At-Home Weddings

You'd think having your wedding at home would be a great way to save substantial sums of money, assuming you or someone you know has one large enough to do the job. But in many cases, the costs can run about the same as a more traditional celebration. That's because in reality most at-home weddings are outdoor weddings without the site fee, and outdoor weddings are expensive. They're also a lot of work.

Charges for a tent run close to a $1,000. You'll have to bring in plenty of lights, chairs, and tables. Catering may be more expensive because it's more labor intensive to deal with food in someone's yard versus a banquet hall with all the facilities right there. Then there are concerns about parking, people messing up the house, and complaints from the neighbors who weren't invited and are irritated about the noise.

Having said all that, the at-home wedding can save money if it's small. You, your family, and your friends can make the food, supply the liquor, and decorate. You can hire a DJ and a photographer or supply these services as well. You'll have no site fees, expensive tent rentals, or big catering bills.

The afternoon ceremony with a tea or cocktail-only reception is very nice for at-home weddings. You'll save on work and costs down the line. Plan a quiet party among your close friends after the reception or head off on your honeymoon. There are many ways to go about at-home weddings, but the most important point is the more traditional you make it the more it's going to cost.

It's worth noting that many wedding consultants feel more couples should be flexible enough to break from costly traditions, especially if the couple can't afford them. A small, non-traditional at-home wedding can be just as splendid as one held at the Plaza Hotel in Manhattan; it's simply a matter of taste and one's ability to be practical. What so often happens is couples go into debt for their weddings and honeymoons because they refused to be flexible and to accept that they couldn't afford the type of wedding they wanted.

Wedding consultants don't believe marriage should go hand in hand with debt. Sometimes, they say, it's better to go with a nice room at a resort after a simple wedding day, to defer the honeymoon if there's no money left for it, and to have a simple wedding with the knowledge that you'll do the big deal at a vow reaffirmation ceremony down the road—many couples do have their big wedding celebrations five or ten years into marriage.

The at-home wedding is often preferred for interfaith marriages by a justice of the peace and can be much more cozy than a chapel wedding.

The Small Wedding

The simplest solution for keeping costs down for the wedding is to have a small one. A wedding with fifty to seventy-five guests is considered small by most industry professionals, and these types of affairs are generally informal or semiformal. They cost 30 to 50 percent less than large celebrations.

The advantages of the small wedding are many. The limited guest list makes it easier to exclude more people with fewer hurt feelings. People understand not everyone can come to a small wedding, and you'll have their best wishes. The moment you plan a large wedding with one hundred and fifty to two hundred guests, everyone will feel entitled to an invitation, increasing the difficulty in deciding whom to exclude.

The small informal or semiformal wedding doesn't require as much expense for attire. The groom can come in a two-piece suit, and the bride can wear a simple gown with few accessories. She can even opt for a nice bridesmaid dress designed in white, eliminating the traditional gown altogether.

The number of attendants is smaller, which means fewer gifts to buy. Plus, it's cheaper for them because they needn't buy or rent expensive formal wear. Flowers needn't be as abundant. The reception site needn't be large. Invitations can be handwritten. The list goes on and on.

The lower costs for a small wedding can enable the couple to pay for a sit-down meal they couldn't afford for a large number of guests. In fact, a small wedding can pave the way for the couple to have a more formal event with more trimmings than they could with a large one. The larger the wedding, the more corners will have to be cut to make it happen when funds are limited.

Finally, smaller weddings don't require as much work and planning, and they can be arranged with less advance notice in most cases. This is a big consideration when balancing the pressures of holding a job with the planning process.

19

All About Wedding Consultants

At first glance, hiring a wedding consultant to handle all the details for your wedding would seem a luxury similar to hiring a person to go grocery shopping for you or to walk your dog. The wedding consultant won't work for free, and his or her fee adds unnecessary expense to the budget categories. Why on earth would a couple on a limited budget even think about hiring one?

The fact is many couples don't have a choice but to hire a wedding consultant. The bride and groom are just too busy to do all the work needed to get the best prices for goods and services, and they lack experience in wedding planning. They don't know which providers in their area are best, reliable, and professional. They don't know how to negotiate for discounts or they're unwilling to try.

This book is all about how you can cut costs and still have a great wedding. Certainly proceeding alone armed with all the knowledge you've gleaned from the text is the cheapest way to go. But if you're unsure of yourself or have so little time that you've gotten a bit depressed reading about all the work involved—all those intricacies, the traps you can fall into—

perhaps a wedding consultant would be a viable option for you to consider.

An ever-increasing number of couples are hiring wedding consultants. The wedding consulting industry grew 11 percent in 1995, and experts expect the trend to continue. Taking advantage of benefits derived from the wedding consultant's knowledge of the business can actually save money in addition to time.

It seems hard to believe that paying extra money for a wedding consultant can shave dollars off the bottom line. But it's true, due to many of the same basic business principles already discussed and how those principles influence how much you pay for goods and services for your wedding.

WHAT TO EXPECT FROM A WEDDING CONSULTANT

The following are some tips from Eileen Monaghan, vice president of the Association of Bridal Consultants, an international trade association for wedding professionals based in New Milford, Connecticut.

Q. What exactly is a wedding consultant and what does he or she do?

A. A wedding consultant is a person in your area who knows the wedding business very well. He or she will work closely with you to help plan a wedding within your budget. After you decide what you expect and want at your wedding, the wedding consultant will take care of everything from ordering the flowers, hiring the photographer or videographer, to arranging all the details for your reception from food to favors.

Sometimes, couples hire a wedding consultant to work just on the day of the wedding. In these cases, the consultant works with all the vendors to ensure everything goes smoothly so you don't have to worry about it. It frees the couple and their families so they can enjoy their special day.

Q. How much does a wedding consultant cost?

A. Wedding consultants charge in different ways. Some have flat rate charges, hourly rates, or they charge a percentage rate. The rule of thumb when figuring out costs for hiring a wedding consultant is that the average price will amount to 10 or 15 percent of whatever the consultant works on. Regardless of how the consultant charges, the bottom-line price for his or her services should be in line with those percentages.

For example, if the consultant handles every detail of your wedding, and the total price for goods and services equals $10,000, the consultant would earn $1,000 to $1,500. Anything more than that would be higher than accepted rates.

Q. You mean I can hire a consultant to handle parts of the wedding planning process, not the whole thing? I'd think the consultant would want to work on as much as possible so they'd get a higher fee.

A. Of course the consultant would like to do as much work as possible. That's just plain good business sense. But no reputable consultant would insist on handling everything if that's not what you want. He or she is there to help you, so if you don't want help with flowers or hiring the limousines, or with other things, that should be okay.

Q. Would reducing the total number of areas the consultant works make hiring one for something I'm not comfortable with affordable?

A. Absolutely. You may not feel comfortable dealing with caterers, for instance. But you feel confident about selecting your gown, hiring the limousine, the photographer, or the band. That's fine. Just be up front when you contact the consultant about what you want to handle yourself and where you need help.

Q. Is it really true that a wedding consultant can save me money? I find that hard to believe.

A. Many couples are skeptical when they hear wedding

consultants can save them money. But it's definitely true.

When you go to a vendor, say a florist, and pay $700 for all the flowers needed for the ceremony and reception, you're not likely to come back next week and order $700 more. The wedding consultant will certainly be back next week or in a couple weeks to place another big order.

This gives the wedding consultant an edge you'll never have. Businesses all want volume and the owners who work with wedding consultants know doing business with them means volume, so they'll lower prices and work very hard to provide quality goods and services because they don't want to jeopardize their relationship with the wedding consultant.

A reputable florist should give you the very best service and quality, but the owner isn't likely to give you the same price discount he or she would offer a consultant who can be counted on to come back soon.

In addition, the consultant is better able to negotiate for extras. Extras thrown in without charge are as good as cash.

Q. Sounds complicated. But I see what you mean. Yet, how does that translate into a savings for me?

A. Reputable wedding consultants will pass along those big discounts to you. They'll do that because they know you'll want to spend the savings on other parts of the wedding which they hope to be involved with. It's a give and take situation. If the wedding consultant saves you money across the board, then he or she should be rewarded for that. You'll come out a winner in a long run.

If consultants are good, they will save you their fee in vendor discounts. In other words, what they charge you will be made up in discounts, so you'll come out even and have the benefit of their advice, their work in planning, and the peace of mind of having your wedding without worrying about every detail.

Q. This sounds too good to be true. What's the catch? There has to be one.

A. There is a catch. Some consultants don't pass along the discounts they receive to the bride and groom. They'll keep the money and add it to the fee they charge you.

Q. That's terrible! It's like they're getting kickbacks. Isn't that unethical?

A. Our association looks down on that practice and strongly encourages members to do what's right for the bride and groom. In the end, though, it's up to the individual consultant and the couple to decide how they work together.

Q. How do I know if the wedding consultant is taking kickbacks?

A. We like to use the word "commissions" not kickbacks. But I suppose it's a matter of semantics. Our point is the consultant works for the bride and groom, not as a salesperson for vendors. The couple should ask if the consultant is getting commissions from the vendors. It's up to the bride and groom to determine if they want to work on that basis.

Some might argue that the consultants deserve to keep the commission, that the added income has nothing to do with the level of service provided for the couple. Of course, we don't agree. But it's worth seeing the other side of the story.

Q. How do I find a reputable consultant?

A. Call us for a referral. Chances are we'll have a member in your area. Or check advertisements for wedding consultants in bridal publications. Get referrals from friends who have used consultants.

Just remember that there are a lot of consultants out there who may not have all the qualifications. Any person can say he or she is a consultant, but are they really good?

Q. How do I know if they're really good? It seems like a gamble to me.

A. When you first contact a wedding consultant, ask if he or she is a member of trade associations, the local chamber of commerce, the Better Business Bureau, and other groups. Ask about his or her educational background specific to the wedding industry such as training courses they've taken prior to becoming a professional wedding consultant.

There is so much training available, most every good consultant will have taken courses. Another point to keep in mind is that the business changes, so ask if they've attended seminars to keep pace with changes in the industry.

But no matter what, you have to have good rapport with the consultant. You've got to feel absolutely comfortable about having the person handle such an important event in your life.

Q. Contracts? Are they important?

A. Without a doubt. You should have in writing how much you're expected to pay for each service and what services will be provided. Everyone's expectations must match. You don't necessarily have to have a formal contract. A letter of agreement will work fine, just so long as it's complete and covers all the details.

Q. When did wedding consultants come on the scene?

A. They've been around forever. In the early days they were for society weddings. Now with our mobile society and everyone working, they're becoming more necessary and more common for middle-income couples planning their weddings.

Names and Numbers

If you would like a referral for a wedding consultant in your area, contact the Association of Bridal Consultants. Phone: (860) 355-0464.

PART II

Saving Money on Your Honeymoon

20

The Sweetest Time

A newlywed couple dances slowly on a moonlit beach to a band playing a romantic song, barely audible in the distance. The trade winds whisper in the palms behind them and the rustle of fronds blends with the gentle wash of the waves. The whole world seems to be spread before them, a vast place waiting for exploration together.

You may set your dream honeymoon just about anywhere: in a tropical paradise, on a cruise ship; in Paris, Rome, London; at a Bed and Breakfast; at a campsite. But no matter where you go, it's scenes like the one described above which create honeymoon magic and romance.

Today honeymoons are as much super vacations as a time for togetherness. After the build-up to the wedding, the honeymoon allows time for reflection and well-deserved relaxation before getting on with the business of life.

In the past, a honeymoon represented all the mystery and desire of love. It let the couple get to know each other intimately for the first time. Brides and grooms of the past were bound by social mores more restrictive than those of today, and honeymoons gave them the chance to kick up their heels at destinations where no one knew them.

Kicking up heels is definitely part of honeymooning, and

has been for centuries. Anglo-Saxons had the habit of drinking honey wine for the first thirty days after a marriage, giving rise to the word "honeymoon." Setting aside time for the couple to be alone together away from the stress of daily life remains a tradition.

For couples on limited budgets who must bear most of the financial burden of the wedding, finding the cash for a honeymoon can be very difficult. Honeymoon budgets vary from practically zero for a weekend camping trip to tens of thousands of dollars for a whirlwind tour of Europe. In the real world, though, most couples spend between $1,000 and $3,000 for the honeymoon.

After all the expenses for the wedding there might be nothing left for the honeymoon. It happens all the time and unfortunately many couples charge the trip instead of putting it off or scaling way back. For the next year they're forced to eat hot dogs and boxed macaroni and cheese to pay off the bills.

It would be a shame to have carefully planned a wedding which stayed within a reasonable budget only to accrue debt for a honeymoon. While a honeymoon is important, it should never lay the foundation for debt. Keeping a cool head from a financial standpoint at this emotional time will help avoid problems and let you have a special honeymoon without going overboard.

As you plan your wedding, also keep the honeymoon tab in mind. What kind of wedding you have plays a big part in determining what kind of honeymoon plans you can afford. A wedding that comes in under budget allows you to channel the surplus funds into the honeymoon; one that goes over steals from the honeymoon. Remember this during the wedding planning phase and you may be less inclined to splurge on a $2,000 gown when you could get another one just as nice for $1,000. Or cater a sit-down dinner of seafood instead of serving chicken, and so on down the line.

If you're fortunate enough to have set adequate funds aside for both the wedding and honeymoon, it's still easy to go over budget on both. Those travel brochures and videos always look tempting. However, you'll still want to plan within the confines of a firm budget. Honeymoons come in all varieties for all budgets. It just takes a little know-how, time for advance planning and booking at the lowest rates, and flexibility in the type of honeymoon vacation you finally settle on and when you go. The following sections of this book will provide you with a wide selection of honeymoon options to consider; you'll find some surprising ways to play the honeymoon game and come out a winner.

CHAPTER
21

What Makes a Great Honeymoon

The definition of what makes a good honeymoon differs with every couple. For some a trip to Las Vegas or New York City, Paris, or London replete with fine dining, floor shows, and shopping holds all the romance in the world. The bright lights, the crowds of people, the grand architecture and historic sites, museums and art galleries, a night out at the theater—these are the pleasures which combine to make honeymoon magic.

For other couples, an urban honeymoon holds no attraction at all. They'd be happier lying around on the beach sipping tropical drinks with umbrellas in them. Or camping, sailing, bicycling, horesback riding; or a trip to Disney World or the Grand Canyon...the list is limitless. But when it comes down to it, the choice of honeymoon destinations ends up being a compromise between the desires of the bride and groom, and the size of their checkbook.

A key ingredient all honeymoons have in common is time alone together away from the fray. Conflicts can occur when the groom wants to play golf all day or the bride wants to shop. The honeymoon should include activities for each of you, and it's okay if you're not glued together at the hip the entire time. The important thing to balance is the time you spend together, and choosing a honeymoon destination which has plenty of activities that you both enjoy will make for happy times to remember forever.

Work out in advance what you both want to do most together on the honeymoon, then consider where and when. If you haven't traveled much, do you want a whirlwind tour of Europe for your honeymoon? It might be better to defer the tour in favor of a few quiet days together at a little inn. The honeymoon of today is a fun-filled time, but on the bottom line it's for the two of you and you should feel relaxed and comfortable. A frenetic schedule could ruin the experience. Build flexibility into your itinerary and don't try to do everything.

Take the time to plan well in advance, and don't feel that you've got to dash off on the honeymoon right after the reception. Many couples prefer a quiet wedding night at a hotel before setting off on their honeymoon the next day. Some wait for the best prices during off-season or for special promotions, which means delay but makes perfect sense. If you get a great dream honeymoon for 25 to 50 percent off by waiting, why not go for it?

CHAPTER
22

On Travel Agents

Travel agents are invaluable assets for leisure and business travelers, and they can be equally so for you. But there are things you should know before dialing your local agent for some advice.

The agent is just that, an agent on commission. Airlines, hotels, resorts, and car rental companies pay a commission of 10 percent to agents who book business. Some industries have cut commissions back and low, ever-changing airfares ensure that travel agenting for your daily bread isn't all fun and games. It's hard work; planning a trip, especially one on the cheap, takes time and lots of it.

Travel agents are more than happy to help you plan your vacation, but don't take lots of an agent's time if you're not serious about going. It's just not nice. When you're set to go, the agent can help get you the best fares, prices on accommodations, travel itineraries, car rentals...you name it, and you usually don't pay a penny for the assistance. (Published "rack" rates are like list prices in retail; the smart shopper never pays the full amount, and agents can facilitate getting deep discount rates. Never believe the prices you see in brochures for that reason.)

Realizing that the agent stands to gain in proportion to the amount of money you're spending, it behooves you to keep an eye peeled for the upsell agents out there intent on steering you into a more expensive package to up his or her take on the deal. Before you walk through the door, come prepared with a pretty good idea of what you want to do, where, and about how much it costs from airfare to accommodations. Ads in travel magazines and big newspapers are a great place to start looking.

When you're armed with basic knowledge of the important facts, it demonstrates to the agent that you're serious and know what you're talking about. Ask about all-inclusive resorts, fly-in packages, air/sea or cruise-only packages for cruise ships, and discounts for off-season. The travel agent should appreciate that you've done a little homework because it'll make the job of helping you much easier; it'll also be less likely that someone will try to snow you.

According to recent reports published in 1995 and 1996 in *Travel Holiday*, travel agents book 80 percent of all air travel and 90 percent of all tours. They know the travel business and have the tools of the trade to get the job done. Use a travel agent for trips far from home where airfare, accommodations, car rentals, and a multitude of other details enter into the equation. It's simply easier to enlist a travel agent than to do it all yourself, and besides, the agent will save you money.

To find a good travel agent, put the word out among your friends and business associates who travel and get a referral. A referral from someone who travels a lot and regularly uses a travel agent means more than a referral based on hearsay for a simple reason: the agent is earning commissions from the frequent traveler and will work harder for you because of your connection to their regular customer. When you don't represent a steady source of income for the agent, or you're not connected with someone who does, the agent may not "shop" your trip, as they say in the travel business, to get the best deal possible. Instead they'll steer you into what won't be the least expensive package but surely will be the easiest to arrange.

Of course, most travel agents don't spurn the walk-in

customer. Just realize the agent will work harder for you if more money is on the line. If you have no connections with frequent travelers who use agents, haul out the Yellow Pages. Look for agents who are members of trade associations such as the American Society of Travel Agents.

Planning Your Own Honeymoon Travel

When you plan your own honeymoon you get to play the role of travel agent. Some people don't have the time for this, nor the inclination. For others, though, travel makes their blood race and planning a trip, especially one as important as a honeymoon, becomes part of the joy during a very special time.

For the urban honeymoon, consider staying at a motel or hotel outside of the city center during the week to get lower rates. You can save 20 percent or more by taking advantage of lower demand for rooms in the suburbs; business travelers often book most of the available rooms in the city. Meals and just about everything else will be cheaper outside the city, too. Go in for day trips and try to take mass transit. Renting and parking cars will eat up savings.

During the weekend, rates drop for rooms in the city center because most of the business travelers have gone home. That's the time to book a room. If you must fly into the city, investigate an airport close by but not the key hub. The airfare rates for the less popular airport could be substantially lower. But one should also check costs of getting from a distant airport—a $25 difference in airfare could well be eaten up in cabfare to the hotel. You could also investigate outfits like a "Cheap Tickets"—ticket brokers who can get good deals on major airlines.

For the resort honeymoon, mid-week packages are the cheapest. Consider a three-day, two-night stay and then a weekend trip to a nearby city. Off-season rates are even more attractive.

If you're going skiing for the honeymoon, your first impulse might be to book a room at one of the ski resorts. Their package deals can be very economical. With a few more calls you could probably find an inexpensive inn or bed and breakfast at 25 percent less. You wouldn't have a heart-shaped tub, but a room with a fireplace isn't an impossibility.

At most ski centers, ski shuttle buses run to and from areas where the less expensive accommodations are located. Driving a short distance to the attraction in a rented car affords a more intimate experience, and the savings in accommodations rates will help offset the car rental expenses and costs at the slopes.

Incidentally, the rates at some ski resorts drop dramatically during the summer. You can go hiking on the trails, visit nearby tourist areas and shopping centers, and get the use of resort facilities at bargain rates.

Consider not staying at a resort, but going to a resort area and renting a cottage for one week. You'll pay around the same price in many cases with the benefit of a nice place versus a cramped hotel room. Or try extended-stay hotels such as Embassy Suites. Also, it's a good idea to call the hotel or motel desk directly instead of going through the toll free number; the folks at the front desk will know exactly what's available, and can often give you a room upgrade or otherwise sweeten the deal. Ask about these options when you call.

To save money, try to select a destination close enough to drive to in your own car; you'll save several hundred dollars on a car rental. If you must fly, investigate discount air carriers. These aren't the big name airlines everyone knows, but the niche of airliners serving the approximately 15 percent of travelers who don't fly the brand jets. You can find discount airlines by calling your travel agent or calling the airport.

Read travel magazines and travel sections in big newspapers to get an idea about the places you fancy. Read the ads, too, and call for information. Also call local and regional chambers of commerce. (Use toll-free numbers whenever possible; sometimes you do have to pay.) Your motor club and state departments of tourism will also gladly help you out. After all, they want you to come on down and spend some greenbacks!

After you've read the materials, you should have a clear idea of key attractions, types and locations of accommodations and restaurants, and costs. Make a number of calls to compare prices, and don't forget to ask about discounts. If you're staying at a resort, study the brochure carefully; if they have a video, order it. Planning your own trip to a regional destination within the continental United States allows you to find the best prices and build flexibility into your trip not possible with organized tours or at an all-inclusive resort.

Taking time to learn about an area in advance helps ensure that you'll get more from the experience when you visit. The flexibility to create your own itinerary, and not get involved in package tours and all-inclusive resorts appeals to the tens of thousands of newlyweds who play the role of travel agent themselves as they plan their honeymoons.

Planning your own honeymoon travel? The important names and numbers listed after each destination highlighted in this book will give you a jump on the legwork. Most of the numbers are toll-free.

24

Free Honeymoons and Weddings

Sounds too good to be true? Who's going to give away a honeymoon or wedding? The answer is that resorts and large hotels who want your wedding business offer free honeymoons as an incentive to get you to close a deal. Many of the larger establishments in urban and semi-urban areas will offer a free honeymoon, a free bridal suite, free airfare, or a percentage discount on honeymoons. These are worth checking out.

Why do some places offer giveaways? The short answer is competition. The travel business, just like the wedding business, is highly competitive and every good business tries to grab as much of the market as possible to keep the cash flowing. Giveaways lubricate the wheels of commerce. The wedding business is integrally linked to the honeymoon business, so it shouldn't be surprising that the savvy couple can turn this relationship in their favor. Keep an open mind and keep a sharp eye out for these special deals.

The price charged for goods and services associated with the wedding may be inflated to help offset the cost of the giveaway. However, these incentive programs are subsidized, and the hotel or resort will try to pass the savings on to you in the form of competitive prices. The honeymoon offered free doesn't cost the hotel as much as it would cost you because they have a special deal going with the honeymoon provider.

It's simple economics: the hotel gets your wedding, plus some wedding guests will also stay for the night. The hotel then sends a steady flow of business to the honeymoon provider, who's thrilled to have you there spending all that extra cash for food, drinks, and activities not covered in the basic package.

Resorts offering honeymoon packages often will throw in a free wedding. They'll do that for the same reason the hotel offered a free honeymoon: volume business. You'll get a free officiant, flowers, dinners for guests, a portrait photograph, favors, and other freebies just for booking you and your guests at the resort. Of course the wedding won't be a lavish affair, but it'll be nice and if you have simple tastes the compromise can be worth thousands of dollars.

If you live in the country or in a suburban bedroom community, giveaways will be tougher to find. These locales often don't support enough industry to ensure steady corporate business or have enough people traveling through to fill rooms. Airports on the fringes of larger cities are busy places where people come together for many reasons. The hotel business thrives, and you're in prime hunting ground for good deals including honeymoon giveaways. Establishments near major airports make a natural spot for a reception, so the couple can hop on the plane without bother.

To find hotels or resorts in your area which may offer free honeymoon and other discounts, study regional bridal guides, newspaper ads in wedding sections, or call local wedding consultants and travel agents.

CHAPTER
25

Destination Weddings

An increasing number of couples are planning small weddings at their honeymoon destinations. In today's fast-paced world, many couples aren't tied to small-town churches or synagogues. They move around a lot and have a relatively small pool of close friends. Planning a destination wedding can shave thousands of dollars off the total cost for both the wedding and honeymoon. The destination wedding is small and informal or semiformal, which reduces or eliminates many budget categories. And, by taking advantage of special offers from resorts, discounts on everything from rooms to meals are easy to get.

Instead of spending $10,000 for a traditional formal wedding, and an additional $3,000 for a honeymoon, why not consider using $8,500 for a dream ceremony and honeymoon at a lovely destination and put the other $4,500 toward a downpayment on real estate or new furniture?

Travel and bridal magazines, and wedding consultants and travel agents have more information on destinations in the United States and in other countries. Some of them will be covered in later chapters.

CHAPTER
26

The Weekend
Honeymoon

Weekend honeymoons can stand in for an unaffordable super vacation. Couples also go on weekend honeymoons if they can't get time off from work. Others have weddings in the off-season and wait for off-season rates at their honeymoon destinations, which sometimes don't coincide. Weekend outings run the gamut from staying at a fine resort hotel or bed and breakfast to hopping a plane for the nightlife at the closest city.

If you're planning to stay in a resort hotel, make sure to ask for special honeymoon packages. You can get them for a weekend. They include lots of perks from free champagne to flowers, and room and restaurant discounts. Call the same place to find out rates for their basic room, and compare the value of what's free with the honeymoon package including the difference between standard and honeymoon accommodations. Sometimes you get a better deal if you keep mum about your honeymoon.

You might consider having your reception at the same hotel you plan to stay at for your honeymoon. You'll have more buying power, which will better equip you to work out a good deal with the management, who may be more than happy to throw in a free room as part of the bargain. Planning a Friday evening cocktail reception, then a stayover at the resort or hotel until Sunday is a cost-conscious way to go.

Check hotels serving corporate customers. They will have banquet facilities and often offer weekend discounts on room rates. You may get an additional discount if the management knows you'll be weekend honeymooning there. Hotels catering to corporate customers in large cities such as New York, Chicago, Washington, D.C., New Orleans, and others will put you close to the sightseeing and you won't get caught up in resort fees. Your stay will be more laid-back as well.

CHAPTER
27

U.S. Honeymoon Destinations

Honeymoon travel destinations in the United States cover virtually every sport, leisure-time activity, climate, and location. You can scuba dive at a coral reef in the Florida Keys or relax at a quaint villa in the Rocky Mountains, shop till you drop in the big cities or worship the sun on a lake or ocean shore. Chances are you'll find interesting destinations to visit not more than a good day's drive from your home.

At the countless resort areas in this country from Palm Beach to the Poconos, you can spend a fortune or, if you downscale, you can enjoy a much less costly honeymoon. As you plan your honeymoon, decide whether you really want the resorty scene with all those heart-shaped tubs and giggly other couples. Pin down where you want the cash to go...luxury accommodations and fine dining; tours, theater, museums; sports like skiing, sailing, golf.

You can find a good match for your tastes in honeymoons anywhere in the United States. Some of the following destinations are honeymoon hot spots; however, most are just popular because of the attractions and scenery. Of course, the list can't possibly cover every destination, but it gives you a good idea of places, prices, and activities.

Seacoast of Maine

Famed for its rocky coast and tasty lobster, Maine is a great honeymoon destination, especially in mid-September when the crowds vanish and prices for lodgings drop. The weather is clear and crisp (not much fog), and honeymoon seclusion is easy to come by. Walk along a deserted beach, share a quiet dinner at a fine restaurant, browse in antique shops, dance the night away at a nightclub...you can do it all in Maine, just a stone's throw from major Northeastern cities.

On the southern coast of Maine, the small, clean city of Portland with its trendy Old Port district offers honeymooners a wide variety of urban pleasures from cultural to culinary. Minutes away is the bustling factory outlet town of Freeport, home to L.L. Bean and similar stores. Portland is just a jump from Old Orchard Beach, a honkytonk beach town with all the trappings. (If you go to Maine in September, you're not likely to put lazing around on the beach high on your list.)

To see the islands in adjacent Casco Bay, hop the mail boat with a picnic lunch. The boat takes you to the larger island communities and in September, with the hordes of tourists gone the sometimes taciturn local inhabitants may welcome you with a smile and some words.

You can do the southern Maine coast on a budget by going in the off-season and staying at one of the many reasonably priced motels outside Portland. Lodging rates per night for double occupancy average between $60 and $80 in the summer months; weekly discounts are common. The close proximity of Portland's airport makes this an enticing, economical fly-in honeymoon possibility (rental car needed) for a long weekend.

Farther up the coast about four hours east of Portland, you'll find Acadia National Park and the resorty Bar Harbor on Mount Desert Island. You won't find easy pickings for bargains; this place is home to zillionaires. If you want to camp in the park, rent a cottage, or even a hotel or motel room in Acadia during July and August, call at least six months to a year in advance. As one of the most scenic parts of the entire East Coast, Acadia is very popular.

Names and Numbers

The Convention and Visitor's Bureau of Greater Portland: (207) 772-5800

Maine Publicity Bureau. Outside Maine in the U.S.A only, call (800) 533-9595. Maine/Canada, call (207) 623-0363

Lake Tahoe

Lake Tahoe, jewel of the Sierras, as it's sometimes called, could also be aptly dubbed the Poconos of the West. While the PR mavens at Tahoe don't tout the region as a honeymoon capital like they do in the Poconos, Tahoe is wedding and honeymoon friendly on a scale as large as the nearby Sierras.

But Tahoe is also much more than weddings and honeymoons. In fact, lots of people go there for reasons not remotely connected with the marriage scene. That's really not surprising since virtually every sport under the sun finds a place at Tahoe, and the alpine scenery is stunning.

Bordered by Nevada and California, Lake Tahoe sits approximately 6,225 feet above sea level nestled in the Tahoe Basin. Majestic mountains tower above the lake, presenting superlative views from the waterfront resorts or nearby summits.

In the summer, people come to Tahoe for the boating and swimming, sunbathing on the beaches, golf, horseback riding, hiking, rock climbing, camping, shopping, and gambling. In winter, they come for the skiing at fifteen alpine and thirteen cross-country ski areas, and other Tahoe staples like fine dining and quality nightlife at the six casinos.

Accommodations range from cheap to exhorbitant. Tahoe can be enjoyed on a budget, however, without much lengthy planning. You could practice the Spartan approach: buy an auto tour tape for $9.95 and slowly drive around the seventy-two-mile shoreline, staying at budget motels along the way with the occasional splurge at a casino. Or you could go all out and spend as much money as you want—diversity is one of the very nice things about Lake Tahoe.

Ski season runs from mid-November through mid-April. Rates are also higher in July and August. It's downright frosty in the winter, about 80 degrees during the day in summer; nights are cool. It's sunny 274 days a year at Lake Tahoe. There's close access to airports.

Names and Numbers

For general information about Lake Tahoe, call the Lake Tahoe Visitors Authority at (800) AT-TAHOE and ask for the travel planner. They also can send you a special brochure all about Tahoe weddings and honeymoons.

Great information on the ski resorts and other activities can be obtained from Tahoe North Visitors and Convention Bureau: (800) TAHOE-4-U.

A wedding planning brochure can be obtained from the North Lake Tahoe Wedding Association: (800) 358-LOVE.

Charleston, South Carolina, and Islands

Located in the low country of the South Carolina coast, Charleston has been a thriving southern city for more than 300 years. Even people who have never been there know Charleston's fame for its antebellum homes, fine restaurants, and, of course, as the site of Fort Sumter where the first shots of the Civil War were fired. Travel and sports magazines often rate Charleston as a top destination for couples and families. It's not a hotbed for honeymooners like some other places, but it's a perfect spot combining romance with the benefits of low prices.

The slow pace of this southern city is one of its more

appealing attractions. You can walk down the tree-lined streets and admire the buildings of a time long past, feeling as if you're also in another era. For honeymooners on a low budget, take the self-guided walking tour together through Charleston. Or splurge on a horsedrawn carriage ride or harbor cruise. Visit the plethora of art galleries, museums, and specialty shops. Relax at a cafe for lunch and in the evening enjoy a fresh seafood dinner and city nightlife.

A nice advantage of this area for honeymooners is plenty of space to find a secluded spot on the beach or in a park to be alone. You're not packed together in a resort with other honeymooners—unless you want that. You're able to enjoy this historic city, beautiful beaches, lots of sports, and you can stay at a resort, a historic inn or hotel, or book a room at the wide selection of budget motels in the area.

Charleston's Islands

Consider flying into Charleston, renting a car, and taking a thirty-minute drive to the resorts on the barrier islands along the coast. Kiawah Island, Seabrook Island, the Isle of Palms, and Sullivan's Island offer boating, swimming, sunbathing, horseback or bicycle riding along the beach, fine dining, tennis, and golf. All these activities are close to sightseeing at nearby plantations and to cultural centers in downtown Charleston.

Golf and tennis are particularly popular among visitors. There are eighteen golf courses in the Charleston area.

The islands in the Charleston area offer an affordable alternative to staying in the heart of the city. Resort honeymoon packages start at around $900 per couple for five days and four nights at peak summer rates and drop as low as $500 in early spring and fall. Private home and cottage rentals are also available.

The average high temperature in January is 61 degrees and 89 degrees in July and August.

Names and Numbers

South Carolina Division of Tourism: (800) 346-3634

Charleston Area Convention and Visitors Bureau: (800) 868-8118

For resort island accommodations and resort information call Ravenel Associates: (800) 247-5050

Poconos

If you want honeymoon paradise, you've come to the right place...the Pocono Mountains, Honeymoon Capital of the World. The folks up in the gentle rolling mountains of northeastern Pennsylvania really know how to show honeymooning couples a good time, and they've been doing it in style since the 1940s when the first couples-only resort opened for business.

As many as 200,000 honeymooners flock to the Poconos every year, roughly 8 percent of the total 2.3 million people who get married in the United States on an annual basis. If those numbers are to be believed, the Poconos hold an irresistible attraction for honeymooners.

What brings all these newlyweds to the Poconos? Lots to do at a bargain price. Also, the Poconos are relatively close to New York and Philadelphia and their suburbs. The easy accessibility brings many who would rather go near than far for the pleasures of all-inclusive resorts, great skiing, horseback riding, boating, swimming, tennis, golf, hiking, and shopping.

The usual way to honeymoon at the Poconos is to select one of the major all-inclusive resorts. The smaller hotels and motels offer good prices, but not package deals like the resorts. Your one-price package covers lodging, most meals, and unlimited use of an array of sports equipment and facilities. Since the resorts cater to honeymooners, they have all the touches important to many couples such as rooms with beautiful furnishings, a heart-shaped tub, and a king-sized bed.

Book your honeymoon at some of the resorts and get a discount on a wedding ceremony and reception. Like Lake Tahoe to the west, and the Caribbean to the south, the Poconos are a prime destination wedding location.

A typical discount wedding package for a ceremony and reception including sixty people, plus a week-long honeymoon costs well under $5,000 with plenty of spending money to spare. A discount wedding package may include the bride's bouquet, the groom's boutonniere, a wedding cake, a thirty-minute photo session, and a buffet dinner reception. Cost: approximately $1,600 to $2,000. Figure another $1,500 to $2,000 for the honeymoon and you see that great, yet still economical weddings and honeymoons are possible.

Honeymoon packages start as low as $600 per couple for five days and four nights. Lower at the smaller establishments. And of course, nobody says you have to stay at a resort...you can plan a quiet, private and wonderfully romantic time in the Poconos yourself, seeking out pretty little inns and towns, and special things to do.

In winter, temperatures are typical of the Northeast—cold and in the 20s much of the time. In summer, 70 to 80 degrees, with some warmer days, is common. Nights are cool. Convenient for fly-in vacation packages.

Names and Numbers

For free travel and honeymoon brochures call Pocono Mountain Vacation Bureau: (800) POCONOS

Niagara Falls

Niagara Falls is located at the west end of New York State on the Niagara River, which drains from Lake Erie into Lake Ontario. It's been a resort town since the mid-1800s, drawing crowds during the summer to view the grandeur of the waterfalls cascading down with an awesome roar.

Ride the glass-enclosed elevator to the observation tower at Prospect Point to admire the view from the top of the falls, and take the *Maid of the Mist* boat tour, a cruise along the base of the falls. Shopping, an aquarium, a theme park, and museums are among the other attractions in Niagara Falls.

Summer is the high season with prices dropping somewhat in late fall and early spring. Winter is quiet, due to freezing temperatures and loads of snow.

In winter, you'll get great prices, if you don't mind the cold. But in the case of Niagara Falls, going the off-season route can be self-defeating. River flow drops to half the 700,000 gallons per second you'll see roll over the top of the falls during the summer. The falls still fall in winter, but they're not as spectacular.

Niagara Falls is home to several wedding chapels. Many hotels, motels, and bed and breakfasts offer special honeymoon packages. In 1996 during the mid-season, one-night, two-day honeymoon packages at a decent hotel ran approximately $150 per couple. A typical honeymoon package often includes the best room in the house, free dinners, drinks, champagne in the room, a gift basket, and a honeymoon certificate for the couple to save as a keepsake.

To cut costs on admission fees, you can buy a New York State Park Attractions pass book. It's full of coupons good for discounts on admission to many attractions.

Names and Numbers

For information on the coupon pass book call Niagara Reservation State Park (716) 278-1770.

For tourism information call Niagara County Tourism at (800) 338-7890. For information about attractions on the Canadian side of the falls, call (800) 563-2557.

Walt Disney World

At first glance, choosing a honeymoon at Florida's Walt Disney World might seem a bit unusual. After all, isn't it for kids? Not if you ask Mickey Mouse. He'd say the magic of the Disney experience is just as much for lovers as it is for kids.

And if you don't believe Mickey, word in the wedding and travel industry has it that Disney World ranks as the number-one honeymoon destination in the United States. Disney officials won't confirm this. However, they do say lots of honeymooners visit every year to enjoy the luxury accommodations, fine dining, and sports activities available at the resorts along with the fun and thrills of the Magic Kingdom, Disney-MGM Studios, and Epcot.

Honeymooners can select from a variety of settings including Disney's Grand Floridian Beach Resort, Disney's Yacht and Beach Club Resorts, Disney's Wilderness Lodge, Disney's Wilderness Resort, and others. Part of the fun of a Disney honeymoon is being taken away to far off places, either based on reality or fantasy, to lose yourself in a world where anything seems possible.

Disney offers a number of four-night honeymoon packages which include unlimited admission to the Magic Kingdom, Epcot, Disney-MGM Studios, Pleasure Island, Blizzard Beach, Typhoon Lagoon, River Country, and Discover Island. The packages offer a range of perks from a photo session with Mickey Mouse to an intimate private meal in your room prepared by a personal chef. In 1996, a low budget Honeymoon Escape package started at around $850 per couple, excluding airfare.

Disney World has also become something of a wedding destination, though with an average of 1,200 weddings a year at the latest count the number isn't staggering. However, the possibilities for theme destination weddings are virtually limitless. Imagine arriving for your wedding ceremony in Cinderella's glass coach and exchanging your vows in the rose garden of Cinderella Castle. It can happen at Disney World.

Packages range from romantic weddings for two to grand traditional weddings involving hundreds of guests. In 1996, the wedding packages started at around $2,500 for an intimate wedding for two. The average price of a Disney wedding for 100 guests was around $19,000.

A small Disney wedding can provide you with quite a lot of

value for your money. You get a beautiful wedding as well as a honeymoon with packages including four-night stays. A Disney wedding isn't cheap if you invite lots of people, but if you scale way back on guests the total price for your wedding and honeymoon can be surprisingly low.

The temperature in Orlando's no fun in summer. In summertime, the average high temperatures hover at slightly above 90 degrees, and it's humid. High temperatures in January and February only hit the low 70s, with lows in the 50s. You pay more for the cooler weather, a consideration to keep in mind.

Names and Numbers

For more information about Disney World, it's best to call your travel agent. Disney doesn't provide toll-free numbers for consumers, so why pay for the call?

If you want to receive the latest information directly from Disney, call the Disney Fairy Tale Weddings Department at (407) 828-3400.

National and State Parks

A "park" honeymoon may not sound all that romantic to the more luxury loving couple. Sleeping on the ground, swatting insects, cooking over a camp stove...no way! But many people love it, and so the camping honeymoon isn't a rarity. Neither are canoing, rafting, mountain climbing, skiing, bicycling, and walking honeymoons. A large number of young honeymooners today fit the work hard, play hard profile, and they often incorporate this in sports-filled honeymoons.

By the way, you definitely don't have to sleep in a tent while seeing the great outdoors and getting a feel for America's natural beauty. You can rent a small RV, a pop-top trailer, or stay in inexpensive cottages and cabins. Find a great spot and stay put, or roam where you choose. If you're already outdoorsy, you may own a canoe, a Sunfish, or windsurfer. Bring the boats along, and the mountain bikes, fishing poles, and cooler. And if you don't own 'em, rent 'em when you get there.

Some Things to Know Besides Not Feeding the Bears

Pleasant day hikes, beautiful scenery, seeing wildlife, getting in touch with nature, swimming, boating, sunbathing…many of the activities offered at resorts are easily obtained at state and national parks at a fraction of the cost of what you'd pay at a resort. Of course, the parks are a tad rugged.

There are all kinds of parks, from primitive to well-groomed. Each have specific kinds of activities available.

Some parks cost money to enter and most charge a small fee for camp sites.

Popular national parks at peak season are almost always crowded.

Tenting, RV, pop-top sites, and park cabins will be booked long in advance, less so with tenting for obvious reasons.

Private campgrounds will be crowded and will be booked well in advance at peak times.

You'll be in a family-oriented atmosphere, though not always.

You may encounter pit toilets or worse, if that's possible. You'll have to cook, at least some of the time, and the wildlife will want leftovers.

Your accommodations most certainly won't include room service and heart-shaped tubs.

Choosing a less famous park enhances the outdoor experience.

Choosing a state park is a good alternative to a busy national park in the same region.

Touring a number of state parks close to home is an inexpensive honeymoon, but it's not for everyone.

Names and Numbers

To find out more about state parks, contact the state's park service. You can find them in the phone book or through information.

To find out more about national parks, contact the Department of Interior, National Parks Service (202) 208-6985.

Foreign Honeymoon Destinations

Mexico

Legend has it that in Guanajuato seeing two lovers lean across a narrow alley to kiss from opposite balconies would scarcely raise an eyebrow. The kissing lovers isn't the stuff of legend, of course, but the narrowness of the alleys where two of the balconies in this colonial city are famous for the cross-alley kiss certainly is.

Most of Guanajuato is an old city, with buildings dating back from the early 1800s. Its intricate street plan makes it an ideal place for pedestrians (some vehicular traffic is routed below the streets in tunnels). A great part of its charm lies in taking long walks along cobblestone alleys which wind among mansions, churches, and public buildings, then suddenly open into a picturesque plaza.

When most people think of Mexico, the glitz of Acapulco or the beach islands of Cancun or Cozumel spring to mind. Or perhaps Mayans and Mexico City...tacos, salsa, and margaritas, sombreros and burrows...mariachi bands and the flamboyant Mexican Hat Dance.

Yet these common associations don't sum up the country's vast diversity. Throughout Mexico's thirty-one states, you'll find something different and exciting. You can visit Mayan ruins, hike through rain forests, tour colonial cities, hang out at a resort, laze on the beach—just about anything a honeymooner could want lies a hop south across the border.

From the Pacific to the Caribbean, Mexico's 6,000 miles of beaches draw sun worshipers to the shore for watersports and night life at the resorts sprinkled in most seaside regions. Among the more popular for honeymooners are the islands of Cancun and Cozumel on the Yucatan Peninsula. Cozumel, Mexico's largest island, ranks as a prime dive and snorkeling destination. The Mayan ruins at Tulum are about eighty miles away.

As with anywhere else, when planning a honeymoon to Mexico you'll need to work out a good definition of what you want before contacting a travel agent. Do you want the usual tourist packages to major hot spots or something different, like a tennis honeymooon at the historic seaside town of Lorento on the Baja Peninsula? (The town's famous for tennis.)

How about a road tour through small towns and fishing villages and off-the-beaten-path cities? Or a honeymoon by rail on the Chihuahua al Pacifico Railway? Order some free brochures from the Mexican government; they're a good place to start.

Mexico has two distinct weather seasons, wet and dry. From June through October, it's hot and wet in Mexico. From November to May the weather is drier. Make sure to ask your travel agent about off-season rates in effect during the least bothersome periods of the wet season in your destination; you could save substantial loot.

You can definitely go to Mexico on a budget. The exchange rate is excellent because of the weak peso, and airfares are often included with discount packages, so getting there costs little. Most recent statistics show Mexico as the number-one foreign travel destination among Americans, with nearly 16 million U.S. citizens traveling south in 1994.

Mexico is expected to continue to be an economical travel destination. For the best rates visit places the Mexicans visit themselves while on vacation instead of resorts which draw lots of foreign tourists. Colonial cities in the interior are much less expensive than places like Acapulco or Cancun. A package during the low season to Cancun averaged around $2,200 per couple for a week.

Entry requirements A passport is highly recommended, though U.S. and Canadian citizens may enter Mexico without one as long as they have some other proper identification.

You will be issued a Tourist Card, which is good for travel in Mexico for as many as 180 days.

Names and Numbers

Before calling your travel agent, order some brochures from the Mexican Government Tourism Office. Call (800) 44-MEXICO.

The Caribbean

Pristine beaches, azure water and sky, the warm sun and soothing trade winds, the beauty of the Caribbean Sea and its green isles has long attracted visitors—from Columbus, who didn't go for pleasure, to Hemingway, who did. For many honeymooners, and other visitors, the Caribbean's main attractions are lazing around on the beach spiced up with watersports, enjoying island sightseeing and shopping, and great meals mixed with night life at a casino or waterfront nightclub.

However, there is much more to do than the usual Caribbean sun and water thing. The more than two dozen countries have fascinating cities to explore, museums to visit, and festivals to join in. Each country, while it shares a common Caribbean link by virtue of geography, offers a diversity of cultures, architecture, foods, and customs. African, Spanish,

British, French, and Dutch influences dominate specific isles, such as French and Creole on Martinique and Dutch on Bonaire.

The Caribbean Sea encompasses Mexico's Yucatan Peninsula, famous for Cancun and Cozumel, and the country of Belize. Heading east off the South American coastline you encounter Aruba, Bonaire, and Trinidad. Winding northward you take in the likes of Martinique, St. Lucia, Montserrat, and Antigua. Turning west takes you through the British and U.S. Virgin Islands, the Dominican Republic and Haiti, Jamaica, the Cayman Islands, and Cuba. The Bahamas are just north of the Caribbean Sea in the Atlantic, but still quite Caribbean-like.

The Caribbean is so vast from a travel and leisure standpoint, it would be impossible to list every attraction. Just a few, aside from the usual fare, include hiking up volcanoes, rafting through a rain forest river, and bicycling less traveled inland roads.

One major problem with the Caribbean is cost. The countries are small and many rely directly on tourism to survive. Prices are higher for everything from a burger and a coke to cabfare. If you go outside the package deals from all-inclusive resorts, tour companies, and cruise ship lines, you could easily spend a considerable amount of money.

You can ferret out good deals for simple accommodations, some with efficiency kitchens, on islands which aren't loaded with resorts and all the other attractions but do offer a nice beach and a couple restaurants, a little town center, a boat or bike rental. This is fine if you plan to just hide away together—read, swim, relax for the duration of the honeymoon. You don't necessarily need a resort package for that.

But for casino action, virtually every sporting activity, lots of sightseeing, shopping, nightclubing, and fine dining you're going to need a much different package than the deserted island type. The Caribbean is packed with all-inclusive resorts from Jamaica to the Bahamas. Check these out for the best bang for the buck. Many offer discount airfares or throw airfares in with the package, and sometimes even tips are included in the base price.

The peak season in the Caribbean runs from mid-December through April. Temperatures average around 70 to 80 degrees, the trade winds blow, and it's life in paradise. From May to October, it's hotter and more humid, and there are hurricanes to worry about. September is most likely to be rainy; it's also one of the busiest hurricane months in the Caribbean.

Here are some surprisingly affordable packages (double occupancy) from peak season in 1996: a seven-night trip to Martinique including round-trip airfare from New York, lodgings, and continental breakfast started as low as $1,600 per couple; a four-day package to the U.S. Virgin Islands including airfare, cottage accommodations, car rental, and other perks, only $1,200 per couple; other packages to Jamaica-based resorts started at around $1,000 per couple.

As you can see, the Caribbean doesn't have to be beyond your honeymoon dreams! Your travel agent can direct you to other low-priced Caribbean honeymoons.

Caribbean Tidbits

More than a dozen airlines serve the Caribbean. If you're paying the airfare, try discount carriers.

You'll have to pay a fee to convert currency back to U.S. dollars, so don't bring home much foreign cash.

A passport is not required at many Caribbean countries, but one is highly recommended.

Taxes on hotel accommodations run as much as 15 percent. Figure on this when planning your budget since many packages don't include it.

Be particularly careful of using phones at hotels—like their U.S. counterparts, most tack on a surcharge, and in the Caribbean it can be as much as 300 percent more than the bill.

Dinner for two at a decent place costs an average of $100; more if you like tropical umbrella drinks.

Water surface temperatures hover at around 75 degrees, and over 80 degrees in summer.

Names and Numbers

To receive a free Caribbean Vacation Planner contact the Caribbean Coalition for Tourism in East Setauket, N.Y. 11733 or call (800) 356-9999.

For a referral to a travel agent with special knowledge of the Caribbean, call the Agency Coalition for Caribbean Tourism at (800) 931-ACCT.

Canada

The great white north, red-coated mounties, friendly folks in lumberjack shirts, sled dogs...these are all stereotypes of our Canadian neighbors. The images may be overplayed, but they do reveal some of the differences between the United States and Canada. Like Mexico to the south, Canada has a distinct personality Americans find very appealing.

More than 12 million Americans visit Canada every year. Those who go for pleasure sample the ski attractions of the Canadian Rockies, the rolling plains of Saskatchewan, the urban pleasures of Quebec's Montreal or the quiet ruggedness of fishing villages in Nova Scotia. British and French influences abound in both the language and architecture, making a visit to Canada a little like traveling to Europe only without the long plane trip and high prices of European countries.

In 1996, the U.S. dollar was worth as much as $1.40 Canadian, an exceptional value. The exchange rates are expected to remain favorable. In the past, airfares were quite high, but lately more direct flights from more major hubs have led to decreases in airfares to Canada.

Single-destination independent and package tours start at roughly $1,000 per couple for seven days, but even lower prices can be found if you shop around or take advantage of special promotions. A 1996 winter promotion for a four-night ski trip to Whistler Resort, British Columbia, including airfare from San Francisco, accommodations (modest), lift tickets and transfers cost only $1,300 per couple at peak season.

July and August are the warmest months with temperatures in the high 70s across most of southern Canada. Spring and fall high temperatures range in the high 50s and low 60s. Winter is downright chilly with low temperatures in many provinces hovering at or slightly above zero.

On Canadian Taxes

Goods and Services Tax   Canada charges a 7 percent tax on goods and services (GST). You can obtain a refund provided you spend at least $100 on eligible goods and services. Refunds aren't issued for goods such as tobacco and alcohol or meals, but are for many other goods as well as for short-term accommodations, a real plus for the traveler on a budget.

Pick up the GST brochure, "Tax Refund Application for Visitors," at Canadian Customs offices and most tourism information centers. The brochure is also available at some Duty Free shops, major department stores, and large hotels. Or you can call Revenue Canada at (613) 991-3346 outside Canada or inside Canada at (800) 66-VISIT.

One important point: keep your original receipts for customs officers because credit card slips aren't accepted as proof of purchases. Also, for accommodations, make sure the nightly price is itemized on the receipt to ensure a rebate.

Provincial Sales Taxes   The majority of Canada's provinces charge a sales tax ranging from 4 to 12 percent on retail merchandise, meals, and sometimes motels and hotels. This is on top of the GST. Some provinces offer full tax rebates for visitors; others don't. Ask about provincial sales tax rebates when you reach your destination.

Take advantage of GST and provincial tax rebates. They can

save you a minimum of 11 percent on many purchases. Add the rebates to the great currency exchange rates and Canadian travel becomes a bargain.

Entry requirements   Same as Mexico's.

Names and Numbers

Contact provincial tourism departments directly for the best travel information on your particular destination. Here are some names and numbers:

Alberta: (800) 661-8888

British Columbia: (800) 663-6000

New Brunswick: (800) 561-0123

Nova Scotia: (800) 565-0000 ext. 580

Ontario: (800) 668-2746

Quebec: (800) 363-7777

Saskatchewan: (800) 667-7191

In addition, major cities also have their own travel and tourism information. Call their tourism offices directly.

Europe

Nothing would seem more romantic than a trip to Paris or London to celebrate the first days of a marriage. But even with the romance that can be found overseas, most honeymooners stick to the United States or head to Mexico or Canada—due to better prices and exchange rates, close proximity, and other conveniences.

According to the most recent statistics from the U.S. Travel and Tourism Administration, when Americans do "journey across the pond," most make a beeline to the United Kingdom, and that goes for honeymooners, too. About 2.5 million Americans visit the United Kingdom every year while a little over 3 million Americans visit France, Germany, and Italy combined.

When traveling to countries with an entirely different take on life, where you don't speak the language and you don't know the customs, stress and other problems often come with the package. The benefits of a honeymoon in such a place may be experiencing the true taste of the exotic, but the more likely choice for a foreign honeymoon destination would be a place where the language, culture, customs, and food are famil-iar...a place like London.

That's a big reason why London is a very popular European honeymoon destination; it's interesting and different, but not so much so that you'll feel like a fish out of water. Have fun and do all the touristy things like sightseeing from the open top deck of a double-decker bus or taking a romantic stroll along the Thames. Linger among the blooms of Kensington Gardens or over a hardy lunch at a pub. Explore Westminster Abby and the Tower of London, and watch the changing of the guard at Buckingham Palace.

After a few days in the city, book passage on the Eurostar "Chunnel" train across the English Channel to Paris. Traveling at speeds up to 185 mph, the Chunnel train can whisk you from London to Paris in just three hours...almost fast enough to make a day trip! The train also can take you to Brussels.

Seeing London and Paris this way could easily be done independently. All you need is a guidebook and a willingness to discover things on your own. Staying at economical places and using a Britrail or Metro pass, you could get away with as little as $80 a day ($300 would be more realistic). Take advantage of low off-season airfare promotions to get you there on the cheap.

Inexpensive tour packages are also available. For example, a low-rate vacation package to London at 1996 winter rates, the Taste of London package from British Airways Holidays, offered six nights in London starting at around $1,200 per couple. The package included airfare from New York or Boston, hotel accommodations, and a continental breakfast. Packages including airfare are often cheaper than plan-it-yourself trips.

Another great discount idea for London honeymooners: the London for Less Card. The card cost $19.95 in 1996 and was good for discounts of 20 to 70 percent at selected restaurants, stores, and attractions. The card is valid for four consecutive days.

Names and Numbers

For more information about traveling to the United Kingdom call the British Tourist Authority at (800) 902-BRITAIN.

For information on Britrail passes call (800) 677-8585 or in New York call (212) 575-2667. Britrail passes must be purchased in the United States.

For information on Rail Europe passes call (800) 438-7245.

Check with your travel agent to see if the London for Less Card or similar discount program is being offered for London visitors. Or call (800) 244-2361.

Biking and Walking Honeymoons

With today's emphasis on keeping fit, walking and cycling have become very popular sports. Not surprisingly, companies offering walking and cycling tours are now common. Perhaps you might consider a more active honeymoon than doing the beach or all-inclusive resort scene.

You can ride or walk through the countryside of Ireland or Britain, Nova Scotia or Vermont, the Caribbean or Baja, and along the way stop at first-rate, quiet inns in picturesque small towns. You can go by yourselves armed only with a guidebook and a sense of adventure. But if you're part of a tour group, your luggage will be transported for you from place to place, leaving you free to ride or walk without hassles. Although there is a fair amount of interaction with others on a packaged bike or walking tour, itineraries usually include choices of activities which allow plenty of time alone.

It might seem that if there's work involved, a bike or walking tour would be cheaper than luxury resorts...well, not always. A professional walking or cycling tour from inn to inn for a week starts at around $1,000 per person in the United

States, closer to $2,000 abroad. Airfare to and from the destination is seldom included in tour packages.

A five-day walking tour around the Bay of Fundy costs roughly $1,500 per couple. Other Canadian packages come in closer to $1,000. Domestically, packages under $500 are available, if you go with a three-day, two-night tour.

Planning your own downscale bike or walking tour is much less expensive. Using your own car or van to get to the destination, your own bike and other equipment, and staying in budget motels will cost around $500 for a week-long tour. (Why not stay at some really nice places, too.) Many couples choose a single destination and plan day cycling or walking trips.

Choose a part of the country you like, contact the tourism department for information about the region, and ask about cycling or walking tours. Brochures on cycling and walking are often available. Sports magazines are great sources for tour companies offering escorted tour packages as well as self-drive, cycle or walk independent vacations; check the classified sections. Travel sections of major newspapers frequently run special features on bike and walking tours. Don't forget to check your bookstore for guidebooks on your destination.

Names and Numbers

Bicycling magazine
2425 Porter Street
No. 3
Soquel, CA 95073

Walking magazine
9-11 Harcourt Street
Boston, MA 02116

Bike and Walking tour companies:

Backroads: (800) 533-2573

Butterfield and Robinson (800) 678-1147

Euro-Bike Tours (800) 321-6060

Imagine Tours (800) 758-8869

Christian Adventures (616) 751-5990

These companies offer free catalogs, brochures, or other information on active vacations.

CHAPTER
30

Cruise Ship Vacations

A warm sea breeze and sunshine, the ocean sparkling all around with no land in sight anywhere...you're on a cruise! You may be sharing the ship with a thousand others, but somehow there always seems to be time for quiet moments of togetherness. Lying around the pool, taking a jog, a great dinner and a show, surely the good life is on the water.

The price for a cruise package covers meals, accommodations, transportation, and entertainment—the key expense categories. Cruise vacations are ideal for the budget-conscious honeymoon couple.

Cruising, particularly in the Caribbean, can be quite affordable and fun. Depending on the season, the cabin, and the ship line, three- or four-day packages on cruises to the Bahamas can cost as low as $1,400 to $1,600 per couple, including airfare. Prices have remained stable in the cruise industry for the last several years and are expected to increase very little in the near future. If you've ever dreamed of a cruise for your honeymoon, this is a good time to go for it.

Cruise ships operate out of Miami, Fort Lauderdale, Tampa, New York, Boston, New Orleans, and Los Angeles. Many packages include airfare, so you don't pay a separate charge to get to the port of departure. Other packages don't come with airfare, but have add-on fares at discount rates. Working with a travel agent who specializes in cruises, you'll find a ship full of amenities you want, sailing to the destination you've always dreamed of.

And, no, outside of a hurricane, you don't usually get seasick on these boats. At 70,000 tons, 800 feet, and at an average price tag of $300 million for the newest in the fleet, the modern megacruise ship is queen of the sea.

CRUISE VACATIONS

Many travelers unfamiliar with cruise ship vacations have to start blind with just the urge to know behind them. They look at ads, call a travel agent, who may or may not specialize in cruises, and they read travel magazines and travel sections in the newspapers. But sooner or later, an expert comes into the picture.

"Admiral" Pat Theberge (he's not a real admiral), president of Cruise Only Vacations in the Boston, Massachusetts, area, has been doing nothing but booking cruises since 1981. He answered some of the common questions about cruising and provided tips on how to make your cruising honeymoon happen even on a low budget.

Q. I've always wondered about taking a cruise. What's it like on a cruise ship?

A. It's very relaxing and enjoyable. You can be alone if you want or you can make friends. If you're active, there are plenty of activities or you can curl up with a book. You've got everything you need, including great food and entertainment.

Q. I've never taken a cruise before. What advice would you give me on choosing one for my honeymoon?

A. A lot of people who have never cruised before think the greatest part is seeing all those exotic ports. The ports are fun, but the ship is the destination. Ports are attractions. When the ship is at sea, it really comes alive; it's something special.

That's why I suggest that honeymooners book a cruise with fewer ports and more time at sea. It's a more relaxing vacation with a balance of two or three days at sea and four or five days in ports.

Then there are cost factors to consider. The cruise with more days at sea ends up costing less than those with many ports on the itinerary. For example, participation in ashore excursion tours runs from $20 to $50 per head for each trip. You'll shop and dine out ashore, all of which costs extra money. Aboard ship, most every bill has been covered.

Also, airfare add-ons can be higher for a cruise with lots of ports on the itinerary.

Q. What's the most popular cruising destination for honeymooners?

A. The Caribbean is the only year-round cruising destination in our area. Most honeymooners, and many others go there.

Many first look at the south Caribbean because the cruises offer lots of ports. We suggest to young honeymooners that a trip through the western Caribbean might be more appealing. It offers plenty of diversity, great snorkeling and other activities. It's also a less costly package than the south Caribbean.

Q. How much would it cost me to go to the Caribbean for a week cruise?

A. That depends on many things. But for someone on a low budget who wants to go on a seven day cruise and is willing to take an inside cabin with two lower berths that convert to a double bed, a cruise to the eastern or western Caribbean including round-trip airfare would cost from $2,000 to $2,500 per couple.

Q. What's this about twin beds? This is supposed to be a honeymoon.

A. For a person on a low budget, taking an inexpensive cabin could make a luxury cruise affordable, and remember, you get all the same meals and entertainment as the guy who paid for an outside cabin with a private balcony on an upper deck. An inside cabin has no portholes or windows, and typically in newer ships the two twin berths easily convert to a double or Queen-sized bed. Outside cabins tend to be larger and have portholes or windows.

The price difference per person between an outside cabin and an inside cabin on the same deck on average amounts to as much as $100 to $150 for a seven-day cruise. When you book an inside cabin make sure the twin beds actually do convert to a double; they don't always in older ships. They're comfortable yet command less of a price.

One last example: an inside cabin on a lower deck for a modest seven-day package would run around $900 per person. An outside cabin on a higher deck with a balcony could be $1,800 to $2,000 per person. There can be quite a spread in price differences. Time of year plays a big part as well as the physical dimensions and level of luxury in cabins.

Q. When is the off-season for cruises in the Caribbean and how much can I save if I take my honeymoon then?

A. Rates drop by 20 to 25 percent in the Caribbean during the off-season. So that's worth checking into from a price standpoint. The cheapest months for a Caribbean cruise are September and October and from late April to the first two weeks of June.

Q. Isn't that hurricane season? I don't think I'd want to be on a cruise during a hurricane.

A. I don't blame you. Yes, those months are smack in the hurricane season. These cruise months still attract plenty of travelers, though. Storms sometimes ruin the party, but not all that often.

Q. How about a cruise to Alaska? Would that be more expensive than one to the Caribbean?

A. Yes, it'd be a lot more costly. Alaska's key season runs from the end of May through the end of August. It's a very limited season and demand for berths is high. That makes fares more expensive. You'll also find an older crowd on Alaska cruises, and fewer honeymooners.

Q.   Okay, not Alaska, not the Caribbean...what about Bermuda?

A.   Bermuda is a beautiful place. A cruise ship can get you there for three days in port, plus four days at sea from New York or Boston starting as low as $800 to $1,200. Cruises are limited from May through October, with June, July, and August being peak for cruise ships.

Q.   Are there other costs I should figure on?

A.   Tips, drinks at the bar, organized shore excursions, shopping or gambling—that kind of thing isn't covered. The package price covers most everything else, so a couple on a seven-day cruise can figure on bringing $500 extra. An average couple will spend $100 on tips for seven days, so that brings it to $400 for extras. If the couple minded their pennies, a total of $500 additional pocket cash would be ample.

Q.   It might be nice to be with other honeymooners like at one of the land resorts specializing in weddings and honeymoons. Are there honeymoon cruises?

A.   No, no line I know of offers a honeymoon-only cruise. But at peak wedding times in the Northeast, such as May through June, plenty of honeymooners will be taking cruises. Most couples get married on Saturdays and leave for the cruise on Sundays, so you'll have more honeymoon couples on Sunday departures than on Saturdays.

Q.   Is a big ship cheaper than a little one, or is a little one cheaper than a big one?

A.   Within each class of ships, you won't find any big price differences among comparable vessels. In other words, as a rule bigger isn't cheaper and neither is smaller. The bigger ships will offer more variety in amenities and activities, but smaller ships can be charming. It's all a matter of individual taste.

Q.   What's the advantage of calling an agent who specializes only in cruises? Won't any travel agent be okay?

A.   The full-service travel agency is okay, but they probably won't have the same level of knowledge a specialist has. It's like going to a doctor. If you knew you had a heart problem would you go to a general practitioner? The cruise-only agency staff will know all the lines and the itineraries. In many cases they'll have cruised on the ships and visited the ports, so they can help you choose just the right ship to meet your expectations.

Q.   Does it cost me extra to use a specialist?

A.   Not a dime. In fact, using a specialist who's up to date on the daily changes in the business can get you better packages at a lower cost than you'd find yourself. Often these professionals are booking lots of business with the various cruise ship lines, and that means they can get lower rates than someone with less buying power. The good cruise agent passes these lower rates along to the traveler in direct savings or cabin upgrades.

Q.   What's the most important advice you can give me about choosing a cruising honeymoon?

A.   If you know you're going to go, do the legwork, make your decisions, and book early. You'll save a bundle on early booking discounts offered by the cruise ship line. And work closely with a travel agent who knows the business and can help you find the right ship with the right itinerary to make the cruise a time you'll always remember.

Names and Numbers
If you want to talk with "Admiral" Pat Theberge at Cruise Vacations, call (800) 445-6541.

To receive a referral to a cruise-only travel agency in your area, call the National Association of Cruise Only Agencies at (305) 446-7732.

CHAPTER
31

Private Boats

If the cruise ship idea doesn't grab you, how about something smaller, say a luxury yacht? Caribbean or Pacific fun in the sun aboard a privately chartered sailboat can be yours for around the same $2,000 to $2,500 you'd spend on a seven-day package aboard a cruise ship. Granted, there are limitations, like having to pay your airfare on top of that $2,500. And, the sailboat cruise won't provide the resort luxury offered on a cruise ship because no matter how hard you try you can't stretch out a 50- to 75-foot boat to 800 feet.

But payoffs exist as well. When you see ports not visited by cruise ships and the accompanying herd of tourists, anchor in secluded coves to swim, windsurf, snorkel, sunbathe, and enjoy gourmet dinners aboard the boat and trips ashore at less traveled destinations, you experience the Caribbean or Pacific at its best.

If you both have sailed before and liked it, you'll have an idea of what makes sailing so special and how it could bring a unique kind of magic to the honeymoon. Yet, sailing isn't for everyone. If either of you have never sailed before and feel apprehensive, perhaps the sailing honeymoon might not be best. Perhaps a powerboat? Houseboats...they're romantic!

Talk to the charter agent about any concerns and remember

that despite their occasional bad moods, the Caribbean and Pacific are usually calm, fine sailing waters. Charter packages in U. S. waters are plentiful; some are inexpensive. In most cases you can charter boats with crews, so neither of you needs a lot of boating experience. By the way, the crew will give you plenty of privacy and pampering when appropriate; they're professionals, and they don't have a shipload of other folks to think about.

How Chartering Works

Go through a charter company. You can find them in the major boating magazines, travel and bridal magazines, as well as through travel agents. Rely on your contact for specific details. But before deciding to go, let's look at a few options.

You can charter "bareboat"—that is, without a crew. As chief cook and bottle washer, you do it all, including sail the darn thing. Provisioning, airport pickups, and other services are available for an extra charge. The prices for the charter depend on the size of the boat, location, and time of year. Naturally, if you live in Michigan, chartering a boat on the Great Lakes would be cheaper than chartering one in the Bahamas; you save substantially by eliminating airfares and other foreign travel add-ons from the equation. Regardless of where, chartering boats, sail or power, also include fees for dockage and electricity, sometimes even for water! Anchoring out eliminates many expenses. The main point is if you have enough basic sailing or powerboating knowledge, its not hard to charter a boat. You simply must show competence, and a command of basic seamanship. With these personal talents you can create a very special "loveboat" honeymoon.

Don't want to sail it yourself? Charter a crewed yacht. The larger crewed yachts are frightfully expensive, way beyond the means of most honeymooners. Price tags of $10,000 a week wouldn't raise an eyebrow for a 60-footer. That's why two or three couples, all of whom know each other, will typically pitch in to charter the big boats. (Having a double wedding? A double honeymoon, perhaps?) Smaller yachts with captains are more affordable.

Some land-based resorts have hooked up with charter companies to offer combination packages to bring sailboat cruising together with the luxury resort attractions so popular among honeymooners. These are worth a look.

For example, The Moorings offers a Yachting Get-A-Way package combining three days and nights of cruising aboard a 50-foot sailboat (you share the boat with one or two other couples) with resort fun ashore for the balance of the week. At the low end in 1996, this kind of package started at roughly $2,000 per couple, excluding airfare. It's not cheap, but it's a unique honeymoon vacation still within reasonable financial limits.

To bareboat charter a 30-foot sailboat for a week during the summer in the Caribbean British Virgin Islands would start at (off-season) around $2,500 including provisions. The price doesn't include airfare, airport transfers or much else. Sometimes you also pay add-on fees for windsurfers and other watersports equipment.

Lower rates can be found, however. For example, all-inclusive crewed yacht packages to St. Martin were starting as low as $1,600 per couple. Again, airfare was extra. The price depends on where and what you get, and who's offering it.

Other options for waterborne honeymoons include luxury barge trips through British and French canals. You can go with a group or charter a small barge just for the two of you and drive it yourself. Domestically, among the most famous (and much less expensive) are cruises on New York's Erie Canal aboard canal boats you operate yourself.

Other cruises (mostly day and evening) are available at major ports such as New Orleans, New York, Boston, and San Francisco, and in many other places as well. Houseboats are romantic and economical, and they're also fairly easy to operate. A houseboat in the Florida Keys for a week typically goes for around $1,500, which includes accommodations, transportation, and even entertainment...quite a value if you like driving houseboats.

Names and Numbers

The following charter companies offer packages for a variety of foreign destinations. Call for specific details on boats, crewed or bareboat charters, charter base locations, and others. Most major charter companies either have in-house travel agencies or have associations with agencies which offer special discount airfare rates for charter customers.

Call The Moorings for current packages such as Yachting Get-A-Way at (800) 437-7880.

Bitter End Yacht Club: (800) 872-2392

Caribbean Yacht Charters: (800) 225-2520

Seabreeze Yacht Charters: (800) 668-2807

Sunsail: (800) 327-2276

For a comprehensive guide to bareboat charters, get a hold of *Sail* magazine's annual survey of the major Caribbean, U.S., and Canada-based charter companies. In 1996, the guide appeared in *Sail's* March issue.

Sail magazine
84 State Street
9th Floor
Boston, MA 02109-2202
Phone: (617) 720-8600

CHAPTER
32

Insurance

Nobody wants to think about trouble, but it's a good idea to stare unpleasant possibilities in the face and take steps to protect the investment you're making in the honeymoon. Before you go, make sure you know what your auto, home-owner's insurance (if you own a home), and health plan will cover.

Check your credit card benefits to see what kinds of coverage you may have such as automatic travel accident insurance or free collision coverage for rented cars (savings could amount to roughly $14 per day in the United States, plus you're covered). If you get extra coverage from the plastic, use it.

And how about the bum deal nature can hand out in the form of hurricanes, earthquakes, and floods? And what about medical emergencies which might cancel or interrupt the honeymoon?

Trip cancellation and interruption insurance coverage will ensure you receive a refund in the event an unforeseen occurrence beyond your control forces you to cancel or interrupt the honeymoon. Definitely purchase it; otherwise if anything goes wrong and you can't go (or while you're there something awful happens, such as the resort burns down or whatever), you won't get a red cent back. Be sure to study the terms carefully and be wary of any pre-existing medical conditions which might crop up to ruin the fun...most policies won't cover pre-existing medical conditions. They also don't cover voluntary cancellations or interruptions.

Trip cancellation and interruption insurance is available through your travel agent or tour providers. The price is worth the peace of mind, particularly for expensive honeymoons. The average fee runs between $50 and $100 for a $1,500 to $2,500 vacation package.

The last, more depressing considerations are medical emergencies or death while traveling. If you're heading far from home and you get sick, medical evacuation insurance will cover the high costs for transportation. Also, you can buy insurance to cover the costs for transportation in the event of death. It's not fun to think about these things, but if anything should happen, the bills could be enormous. Get the insurance.

CHAPTER
33

Passport Basics

In Canada and Mexico, and many Caribbean countries, U. S. citizens aren't required to carry passports. A notarized birth certificate combined with valid photo identification (driver's license) does the trick in most cases.

Travel experts advise bringing your passport anyway because it's rock-solid proof of identification and U.S. citizenship. However, if neither of you has passports you may consider saving the money for them if you travel to Canada, certain places in Mexico, and the Caribbean; talk with your travel agent well in advance of the trip to determine whether you should pay for passports.

If neither of you has a passport, you'll have to come up with $130 for the documents plus photo charges of approximately $20 for both of you. A U.S. passport costs $55, plus a $10 processing fee. It's good for ten years. Typically, it takes four to six weeks to receive a passport.

You can apply for a passport at county passport offices or go to major passport offices located in large cities. Obtain an application and passport photos before going to a passport office to process the application.

When you go, bring the completed passport application and proof of citizenship (your old passport, naturalization papers or an official birth certificate with the raised seal). Also bring your driver's license or other form of identification.

Have your passport pictures taken professionally at a one-hour photo shop. The cost is usually around $10 for the two required identical photos (two inches square). The photos must be taken within the last six months of applying for the passport.

You can find county passport offices in your phone book or through information.

Names and Numbers

For general passport information call the Federal Information Center at (800) 688-9889.

CHAPTER
34

Basic Travel Tips

Take advantage of Gold Card discounts or free insurance offers for car rentals.

Use your credit card instead of paying cash in foreign countries. This guarantees you'll receive the best exchange rate.

Exchange rates differ from bank to bank, and are least attractive at airports and other key centers for travelers.

Get a credit card which has a free air miles program. Charge and pay off bills for the wedding on the card, and you could get free airline tickets for your honeymoon.

Use your frequent flier miles, if you have them.

Use a travel agent and book months in advance.

If you have a flexible schedule, wait for a special promotion package for your destination. Special promotions save 10 to 20 percent, sometimes more.

When booking a hotel or motel room, ask if they have a corporate discount plan. You may get the discount just by asking for it.

Take advantage of auto club discounts or those from other organizations on rooms and services.

Sometimes flying to a less popular or busy airport and renting a car saves money. Demand for flights to major airports boosts rates.

Airfare rates are lowest on Tuesdays and Wednesdays, and a Saturday stay-over can mean extra savings.

Discount airlines can save you substantial sums of money. Ask your travel agent about them or call your local airport. Also inquire about consolidators. They buy up seats in bulk and sell them at deep discounts, usually through travel agents only.

Buy a Britrail pass for rail travel in the United Kingdom. A variety of Eurail passes are also available for travel to many European countries. Buy the passes ahead of time in the United States. Your travel agent can help. Rail trips are great ways to have inexpensive honeymoons which cover lots of ground.

If planning a rail or driving tour, ask your travel agent about airfares allowing you to depart from another city. You may pay less in the long run because you won't have to return to your initial destination, and the convenience factor is worth considering.

Many U.S. and foreign cities offer discount books good for lower rates on hotels, car rentals, restaurants, museum admissions, and other attractions. Always ask about these.

More Cheapskate's Books
From Carol Publishing Group

The Cheapskate's Guide to Las Vegas (Updated) by Connie Emerson
Sound advice on how to get maximum satisfaction with minimum expenditure. Complete with money saving information on • Dining • Shopping • Top attractions and entertainment • Gambling • And much more. $10.95 paper (#51844)

The Cheapskate's Guide to London by Connie Emerson
Tips on the best discount shopping, attractive low-priced restaurants, deals for theater tickets and bargains on hotel and bed-and-board accommodations. The book also offers detailed information on the city's parks and museums. This book will give you all the information you need to have a four-star vacation at a one star price. $9.95 paper (#51655)

The Cheapskate's Guide to Living Cheaper and Better by Leslie Hamilton
From decorating and repairing the home to maintaining the value of your car to tips on cheaper vacations to knowing when to sell stuff to get the best price, this book helps readers reduce cash flow without lowering their standard of living. $9.95 paper (#51795)

The Cheapskate's Guide to Paris by Connie Emerson
Readers will learn how to get maximum value for their francs, on everything from shopping to sightseeing to entertainment. Including tips on how to take advantage of senior citizen discounts as well as places to entertain the children, this book offers a key to parks and museums and reveals which attractions offer free admission. $9.95 paper (#51736)

The Cheapskate's Guide to Rome and Venice by Connie Emerson
From discounts on airline rates to the best hotel rates (both in season and out) this book offers advice on how to tour the Eternal City, plus tips on shopping, dining, and which attractions are cheap or free. $9.95 paper (#51850)

The Cheapskate's Guide to Vacations by Steve Tanenbaum
Four-star vacation at one-star prices are just pages away. This guide offers pointers on unlocking free travel dollars, including countless frequent-flyer miles (without even taking a flight!), hotel and dining discounts, and the cheapest deals on tours and cruises. $12.95 paper (#51832)

The Cheapskate's Unauthorized Guide to Walt Disney World
by Mike Lewis and Debbi Lacey
Budget-conscious travelers will learn where to stay, eat, and shop, in addition to what to see when in order to avoid the crowds. $9.95 paper (#51877)